How to Clicker Train Your Cat

How to
CLICKER
TRAIN
Your Cat

A Step-by-Step Guide to Teaching New Skills and Fun Tricks in 15 Minutes a Day

STEPHANIE MANTILLA

callisto
publishing
an imprint of Sourcebooks

Copyright © 2021 by Callisto Publishing LLC
Cover and internal design © 2021 by Callisto Publishing LLC
All images used under license iStock
Author photo courtesy of CJ Mantilla
Cover Designer: Julie Schrader
Interior Designer: Patricia Fabricant
Art Producer: Samantha Ulban
Editor: Samantha Holland
Production Editor: Mia Moran
Production Manager: Michael Kay

Published by Callisto Publishing LLC C/O Sourcebooks LLC
P.O. Box 4410, Naperville, Illinois 60567-4410
(630) 961-3900
callistopublishing.com

Printed and bound in China
OGP 2

For CJ, who is a zookeeper at heart.

CONTENTS

INTRODUCTION

During my 12 years as a zookeeper, my favorite animals to train were cats: cheetahs, tigers, and leopards—oh my! Working at the Houston Zoo, I learned how positive reinforcement training could benefit both the animal and veterinary staff; for example, by teaching big cats to be willing participants in their own medical care. Without the ability to train lions and tigers to voluntarily come over to get shots or have blood drawn from their tails, we would have to resort to anesthesia, which can be very stressful for the cat. Not to mention the stress involved in making a large cat unhappy!

Most people have never thought about training their house cats, though. There's a common misconception that cats are stubborn and impossible to train; in reality, they are just as trainable as dogs. In fact, some common traits of cats make them the best training subjects.

One widely held belief is that cats are lazy and sleep most of the day. Actually, cats naturally conserve their energy and are active in shorter bursts, usually when hunting. Because of this, cats do very well with fast 5-minute training sessions and are motivated to work for food.

Cats are also independent. With positive reinforcement, this independent behavior makes training easy and fun, and your cat will enjoy participating. Conversely, if you punish a cat, they will simply walk away and not come back. Building a positive relationship with your cat will only improve their overall behavior.

Additionally, cats are more agile than dogs, making them more capable of performing acrobatic tricks involving climbing and jumping in smaller spaces, such as in your home or apartment.

The easiest way to use positive reinforcement and train your cat is with clicker training. A clicker is a small handheld device that makes a "click" sound every time you press the button. Clickers are relatively inexpensive and easy to stock up on and stash around your home or keep in your pocket for quick access. The unique clicking sound clearly communicates that your cat did something right and will be rewarded with a treat (more on this later). You'll continue using the clicker after you've taught your cat a skill to remind them of the desired behavior. It's quick and easy to use, making it perfect for short bursts of training. Communicate desired behavior, click, and treat—that's it!

This book was written to help you build a stronger relationship with your cat, and to reverse any negative behaviors you may be experiencing with your feline friend. You'll discover various exercises to train your cat in all kinds of ways, from practical skills and behavior solutions to fun tricks.

As a zookeeper, I trained lizards, parrots, primates, cheetahs, and everything in between. Throughout my education training animals, I completed an advanced certificate in Behavioral Husbandry, a holistic field that encompasses making sure an animal's social, physical, and mental needs are met in their daily care. I've also completed training at top US animal facilities, including Disney's Animal Kingdom and Chicago's Shedd Aquarium.

I now focus my attention on training domestic cats and dogs, helping people strengthen their relationships with their beloved pets. I love animals, which is why I wanted to write this book. I'm excited to give you the foundation to understand how to clicker train your cat and ultimately enrich the bond you share with your cuddly companion.

HOW TO USE THIS BOOK

This book is divided into two parts. In part 1, you'll learn the basics of cat behavior and communication. To make progress in training, it's important to understand what your cat is trying to tell you and how their training differs from that of other animals—even other cats. Human behavior is very different from cat behavior, so you'll learn what your cat is communicating to you with their unique body language expressions and vocalizations.

We'll wrap up part 1 with an overview of the basics of clicker training. By the end of chapter 3, you'll understand the benefits of clicker training, what tools are necessary to get started, and how to build your training skills, even in the face of common hurdles. I've also provided a template for a training session log so you can keep track of your cat's progress.

In part 2, we'll launch into the training plans. Each chapter in this section contains various exercises and skills to teach your cat. Make sure to start with chapter 4, as it covers the practical and most important skills you'll need for training. Try not to skip around when learning these skills and behaviors, as they provide the foundation for your cat's behavior and ability to learn more fun skills later on.

Once your cat has a solid footing with their training, they will be less likely to get confused or frustrated as they learn more difficult tricks. These basic behaviors are also a great way to pull a timid or skittish cat out of their shell. Chapter 5 will help you solve common behavioral issues, while chapters 6 and 7 will cover fun games and cool cat tricks.

I truly hope the exercises in this book help you train your cat important (and fun) skills. By training your cat, you are creating a lasting bond in which you and your cat will understand each other on a deeper level. Let's dive in!

PART 1

Learning the Basics

To effectively train and bond with your cat, you need to understand their behavior. While each cat is unique, all cats exhibit some similar behaviors, including how they communicate and learn various skills. Throughout this section, we'll cover the basics of cat behavior and communication, plus the essentials of clicker training, before you start practicing with your own cat. Here we go!

CHAPTER 1

UNDERSTANDING CAT BEHAVIOR

This chapter serves as a crash course on understanding cat behavior and how cats have evolved into the companion animals we know and love. Understanding cat behavior is essential, not only for training your cat but also for recognizing whether or not your cat is comfortable during training. Learning more about where your cat came from and how they behave will strengthen your connection and build a better training relationship.

How Your Cat Came to Live in Your Home

Domestic house cats can be traced back to the African wildcat, which is still found across Africa and parts of Asia. Small in stature, this species of cat is light gray and tan in color except for some white on their belly and dark striping on their tail and legs. If you visit Africa or parts of Asia today and see one in the wild, you may not even notice a visible difference from today's typical tabby cat, except this wild cat has a slightly longer tail and legs. Their behavior is even similar to a domestic cat's—they're solitary, meaning they don't travel in packs, and they hunt small rodents and birds. I'm sure you've seen your own cat catch bugs or try to hunt while peering out your windows.

Research indicates cats were first domesticated in the Fertile Crescent (an area in the present-day Middle East) around 12,000 years ago. This lush agricultural area stretched from the Tigris and Euphrates rivers to the Nile River. As the population on the land grew, so did the population of pests, such as mice and rats, attracting wildcats to the area to hunt and putting them in close proximity with humans.

The ancient Egyptians recognized the cats' efficient hunting skills. They witnessed cats protecting their homes from scorpions, snakes, and rodents, so they made them part of the family. In fact, the ancient Egyptians came to worship cats and considered them magical beings. Harming them was punishable by death.

Although African wildcats are feral, their kittens who grew up around humans eventually became comfortable with and even affectionate toward humans. This led people to provide cats with a safe place to stay and furthered the human-cat bond. Essentially, cats domesticated themselves by moving closer to humans so they could take advantage of an easy food source.

Using what we know about cats allows us to train them more efficiently:

🐾 Cats have a high prey drive and are easily motivated by food.

🐾 Their affection toward humans is typically in small bursts, which makes short 5-minute training sessions perfect for holding a cat's attention.

🐾 Cats are opportunistic and smart enough to figure out what you're asking them to do in order to get easy food.

KITTY FAQ: "ARE CATS ACTUALLY DOMESTICATED?"

Scientists often debate whether house cats can be considered domesticated. The leading consensus is that cats are actually only semi-domesticated, since there's not much genetic difference between house cats and their wild counterparts. House cats simply evolved to be more tolerant of humans and other house cats, while wild cats are still completely solitary.

On the other hand, dogs that were commonly found wandering around in villages were purposefully domesticated to help humans perform certain tasks, like herding or hunting. Cats largely haven't undergone this type of selective breeding for behavior, so their behavior is primarily unchanged. However, this lack of selective breeding can be helpful in training since cats are still heavily prey-driven. Cats can be motivated to train by using food, and they enjoy the mental stimulation they would have received when hunting.

THE CAT'S CULT OF PERSONALITY

It's well known that cats prefer to be independent. Compared to dogs, who are often described as unconditionally loyal, cats require more work to gain their approval. One wrong move and you could be out of your cat's good graces.

While a cat's apparent aloofness does hold some merit (who hasn't been snubbed by their cat?), a lot of their perceived unfriendliness has to do with the difference between how cats and dogs were domesticated. Dogs were bred over the years to perform various jobs and to adopt certain personality traits, but cats were utilized for pest control. As long as they kept the pest population under control, their personality didn't matter.

Most cats exhibit many of the same personality traits, but not every trait will apply to every cat. Knowing which personality traits your cat possesses will help you optimize your training sessions so your cat is comfortable and capable of being trained. Read on to see which of the following traits you can identify in your cat.

CURIOUS

Curious cats are often seen exploring and getting into things around your home. Whenever anything new enters the scene, like a new chair or a new arrangement of furniture, your cat will be right there to check it out. Curious cats tend to be outgoing and don't let fear hold them back.

This explorative spirit can be leveraged to introduce different items during training, such as stools, tunnels, and hoops, without scaring your cat. You'll want to allow your cat to explore the items first, but they'll generally be less hesitant to use them due to their curiosity.

IMPULSIVE

Impulsive cats act and react quickly without thinking. This can be both good and bad in a training scenario. You'll want to achieve a level of predictability so you have a general idea of the training steps and how your cat is going to react.

An impulsive cat may throw your training plans out the window if they don't react or progress to the next training step as you had anticipated. You may need to problem-solve if this happens. On the other hand, impulsivity can be good. Your cat may exhibit fun and unique behaviors that are more difficult to train, like air acrobatics or jumping to the top of a door.

SKITTISH

Skittish cats are excitable or easily scared. This behavior could result from a loud noise or unexpected movement. It may take more effort to build a positive relationship with a skittish cat at the start. For example, you may need to slow down your hand movements or muffle the sound of the clicker.

Skittish cats are more likely to hide or run away when something unexpected happens. For training, it's important to give your cat a place to run to or hide where they feel safe, but not somewhere that will be difficult to coax them out of.

INDEPENDENT

Independent cats feel confident being out with you but don't necessarily need you for anything. They most likely won't follow you around the house or beg for your attention. This trait is great for training, since an independent cat is confident enough to be comfortable around you.

Independent cats are still motivated by food but may prefer not to get a lot of praise and physical affection. Keep this in mind when training to avoid creating an overwhelming or negative experience for them.

FRIENDLY

Friendly cats want to be around people. They show affection through head-butting, purring, and coming over to be petted. Friendly cats are easier to train than skittish cats because they want to be around people.

However, friendly cats have a tendency to come to your lap or beg for pets more often, which can make it challenging to keep them focused on the training session. This type of cat may be more motivated by praise and affection than treats.

KITTY FAQ: "HOW DO INDOOR CATS BEHAVE VERSUS OUTDOOR CATS?"

Indoor and outdoor cat behavior doesn't vary much, but there are some environmental considerations. An outdoor cat will likely be more aware of their surroundings and on the lookout for predators. There may be more distractions outside with flying bugs, birds, cars driving by, and other elements.

Both indoor and outdoor cats should be trained where they feel safe and secure. How your cat expresses themselves during training may change, depending on how comfortable they feel. Think about this: If your cat is outside, they may rub against your legs to be friendly but may not flop onto their side to be petted due to potential vulnerability from attack in that position.

Many people think of outdoor cats as skittish and indoor cats as affectionate; however, the opposite can be true. Their behavior has more to do with their prior experiences, so consider whether they'll feel more comfortable training inside or outside. If your cat isn't comfortable somewhere, don't force it. Work within their comfort level.

DOMINANT

Dominant cat behavior is important to understand, especially in multi-cat households. The dominant cat is usually the one who rubs their face on items, "claiming" them as their own, and takes toys away from the other cats. They may also act with aggression toward other cats when food is involved.

When training more than one cat, it's important to understand which one is dominant. The dominant cat may interrupt the training sessions of your less dominant cat(s) and try to steal their rewards. You can avoid this situation by taking each cat to a separate room and training them one-on-one.

SUBMISSIVE

A submissive cat will show their submission or compliance by flattening their body to the ground and flattening their ears. In a multi-cat household, this type of cat may also be skittish.

During a training session, a submissive cat is going to keep track of the dominant cat, so they can move out of the way if the dominant cat comes around looking for something the submissive cat has, like a bed, toys, or food. You can help this underdog (or "undercat," in this case) build up their confidence in training by taking them to a room to train one-on-one. Understandably, this cat will be able to focus better when they aren't constantly worried about the other cats.

Cat Behavior by Age

As your cat ages, their behavior will change. Just like us, a cat's experiences and developmental milestones will change as they transition through life. In this section, we'll go over the main differences you'll see as your cat ages, and how different life stages may affect training.

KITTENS

Play is a huge part of a kitten's life and serves an important role: It keeps kittens active and allows them to practice their hunting skills before they would typically need to rely on them for survival. This desire to play emerges at around 10 weeks of age, when they start to wean.

Once your kitten isn't focused on nursing and shows a little more independence, you can begin building a positive training relationship with them. Start by teaching your cat boundaries around not attacking your hands and feet (see exercises, pages 72 and 74). Instead, redirect them to toys, scratching posts, cat trees, or other appropriate outlets.

Also, get your kitten comfortable with being handled. Take them to different rooms to help with future training. Use feather toys to entice your kitten to climb on stools and follow you around your home. Keep in mind: Feeding kittens too many treats or restricting their diet will inhibit their growth. Kittens grow quickly and need all the calories and nutrients possible. Too many treats and they can become nutrient-deficient; too little food and they won't grow as they should. Both scenarios can cause medical problems, including stunted growth and digestive issues.

Your kitten's personality will determine when you are able to start formally training them (or continue light training, like establishing boundaries). When starting out, I suggest teaching your kitten the first seven behaviors in chapter 4, as well as the behaviors in chapter 5 about not biting hands and feet.

ADOLESCENT CATS

Cats are considered adolescents between six months and three years old. A cat's body is fully grown around their first year, but their mind and behavior continue to develop and mature until about age three. During this time, your cat will become even more independent and start testing the boundaries you've set. If you haven't started training your cat, this is the perfect time to start.

During adolescence, your cat will be more motivated by food and have a better attention span than in the early kitten months. Consistency with training and expectations of your cat is important at this stage. Cats thrive on routine, so training consistently two or three times a day will give you and your cat something to look forward to. Now is the time to get all of the basic behaviors down from chapter 4, solve any behavioral problems you're having (chapter 5), and move on to the fun tricks and games in chapters 6 and 7.

ADULT CATS

Your cat is an adult when they are between three and ten years old. At this age, they will be fully grown, their mischievousness will have died down, and their personality is pretty much set.

There is a common misconception that you can't train older animals, but many adult cats will become more affectionate or outgoing after they start training regularly. It's never too late to begin training your cat. Even if you've had them since they were a kitten, training can start anytime.

SENIOR CATS

Senior cats are typically age 11 and up. During this stage of life, senior cats may experience certain health issues or bodily limitations that make doing advanced tricks too difficult. An example might be training a 13-year-old cat to jump through a raised hoop. This cat may not have the muscle strength to jump as high anymore, nor the agility to land safely without injuring themselves. You can protect your cat by thinking about training from your cat's perspective and keeping expectations reasonable.

However, your elderly cat can be taught all the practical behaviors from chapter 4 and trained to solve behavioral issues from chapter 5. It's the tricks and trainings from chapters 6 and 7 where you'll need to consider if your cat has any limitations that would make those lessons uncomfortable or risky for them.

CHAPTER 2

CAT COMMUNICATION 101

Have you ever wondered what your cat is trying to tell you? Knowing how your cat communicates will make all the difference with training and bonding. This chapter offers an introduction to the art of cat communication, with each other and with humans. You'll learn to decode what your cat is trying to tell you and acquire some tips so you can communicate back with them.

How Cats Communicate with You

Cats communicate in three ways: through body language, sounds, and facial expressions. By understanding what your cat is trying to tell you, you gain valuable insight into your cat's state of mind. And by being able to decipher your cat's behavior, you're on your way to becoming a good trainer.

During a training session, it's important to know if your cat is comfortable so they can properly learn the behavior you're working on. If your cat is nervous about being near your dog or in a different environment than they're used to, they'll be distracted, which can result in a negative experience for both you and your cat.

BODY LANGUAGE

Body language refers to the behaviors and positioning of your cat's body, including their back, fur, legs, and tail. Body language is an excellent indicator of their mood, and it's one of the first you might notice while training. In this section, we'll cover the most common postures, tail positions, and actions that cats display and what they mean.

It's important to see the big picture when looking at the body language of your cat. Similar postures or tail positions can mean completely different things depending on the sounds and facial expressions that go along with them.

POSTURES

A cat's posture is one of the easiest body languages to spot since it's the most obvious. Cats will commonly reveal intense emotions like fear, happiness, or security through the position of their body. When training, you'll want to see a neutral, attentive body posture.

Here are some other postures you may see:

Belly up: A cat lying belly-up is exposed and vulnerable. If your cat is doing this, you can be sure they feel comfortable and safe around you.

Crouched down: A crouching body position indicates fearfulness or anxiousness. Your cat is trying to make themselves appear small and is telling you to back off. This posture is often paired with sideways ears, dilated pupils, and their tail wrapped around their body.

Arched back: When you think of cats during Halloween, this is that cat. An arched back is a sign of aggression and is usually paired with a puffy tail and hissing.

READING THE TAIL

Your cat's tail is mainly used to assist them with balance. It acts like a rudder and counterweight when they're climbing and balancing. But your cat's tail is also an excellent indicator of their mood. Cats can communicate confidence, fear, and even irritation through their tail. Let's learn how:

Flagpole tail: A tail standing straight up with flat fur indicates confidence, alertness, or happiness. However, if the tail is in this position but puffy with fur sticking out, this indicates fear or aggression.

Question mark tail: A tail straight up with a curve at the end like a question mark means your cat is playful.

Tail low to ground: If your cat's hindquarters are crouched and their tail is low to the ground, this indicates insecurity, anxiety, or pain.

Quivering tail: When your cat's tail is straight up and quivering as if it's vibrating, this shows excitement and happiness. But watch out! This is also an indicator your cat is about to spray urine if they're not spayed or neutered.

Swishing tail: When the end of your cat's tail is swishing side to side while sitting, this expresses mild irritation, or they're hunting and playing. If their tail is thumping on the ground and the swishing is more pronounced, anger and greater irritation are at work.

Wrapping tail around human: If your cat comes over to you and wraps their tail around your leg, this is a friendly greeting.

Wrapping tail around themselves: If your cat is crouched down on all four feet and has wrapped their tail around their body, they are expressing discomfort, pain, or illness.

ACTIONS

Cats communicate with each other in much the same way they communicate with us, including behaviors like grooming, stretching, and head-butting. Many of these behaviors can be used with the trainings in part 2. For example, you're trying to train your cat to flip something over. If they're already digging in their litter box, you can leverage this digging behavior to have your cat press a lever that flips an object over. A cat's inherent behaviors are great building blocks to train them to do more fun and unexpected tricks.

Stretching: A cat stretching in front of you feels safe and relaxed. They've let their guard down and are at ease being more vulnerable.

Head-butting: Head-butting is actually an affectionate behavior in cats. It's also a way for your cat to put their scent on you, claiming you as "one of their own."

Rubbing against you: Rubbing is another way your cat transfers their scent to you. It is a loving behavior which means you're part of their group.

Licking/grooming: Cats groom themselves to keep clean, but they are also known to lick their favorite people. When your cat licks you, they're removing other scents while depositing their own, expressing their affection.

SOUNDS

In this section, we'll explore the most common noises cats make and the most important ones to understand for training your cat. For example, you'll want to know when your cat is stressed, uncomfortable, upset, or afraid because trying to train them at that point may do more harm than good. You only want to train your cat when they're comfortable and calm.

MEOW

This quintessential cat noise is the most common vocalization you'll hear your cat make. It can mean a variety of things like trying to get your attention or wanting to draw attention to something else. Your cat could also be asking for food, wanting to play, or looking for you to pet them.

PURR

A purr sounds like a rhythmic vibration from the cat's throat. Purring sounds are made during both happy and stressful times and convey strong emotions. Cats will often purr while being petted or cuddled, but a cat may purr when they're extremely stressed. In stressful situations, your cat's purr is like a defense mechanism that helps keep them calm.

HISS

A hiss is a sharp, threatening noise made when your cat's mouth is open and teeth are bared. Hissing is a defense when your cat is scared or uncomfortable. It can sometimes escalate to a spit, where your cat exhales sharply while closing their mouth, expelling saliva. This sound is an indication that your cat wants to be left alone.

GROWL

Growling is a threatening vocalization, typically with a low, rumbling frequency. Your cat may be lying down in a defensive position to make themselves look small. This warning sound communicates that your cat feels scared or threatened and wants to be left alone. Growling can escalate to hissing, biting, or attacking.

KITTY FAQ: "WHY IS MY CAT SO CRAZY SO EARLY IN THE MORNING?"

Does it seem like your cat has endless energy early in the morning? Cats are *crepuscular*, which means they're most active in the morning and evening twilight hours. This schedule evolved because midday is generally the hottest part of the day. Cats sleep 12 hours a day, so it makes the most sense to be awake to hunt when it's cooler out and their prey is active. Cats have great eyesight in low light, improving their chances of catching prey during these times, as well.

Unfortunately, your cat at home didn't get the memo that they don't have to worry about hunting for prey. They instinctually want to hunt and play during this time. You may even have gotten your feet attacked while you were peacefully sleeping. To avoid this rude awakening, you may need to close them out of your bedroom when they start getting energetic. Another way to prevent them from waking you is to set an automatic feeder to dispense food during the time they're normally zooming around. This may distract your cat enough and fill them up so they move their energetic bursts to slightly later in the day.

CHATTER

A cat's chatter sounds like a repetitive "eh-eh-eh" noise in a high-pitched frequency, made with their mouth open. Your cat might chatter when they are staring at prey, like a tempting bird outside the window. This sound occurs when your cat can't reach their prey. It indicates excitement or frustration.

TRILL

The trill sounds like a mix between a meow and a purr. This high-pitched, chirp-like noise is made while your cat's mouth is closed. It's an affectionate greeting between mother and kittens but is used as a friendly greeting for humans as well.

YOWL

A yowl is a long, drawn-out, intense, and ongoing meow sound. It's a threatening noise your cat will loudly make as a last-ditch effort before attacking. Yowling is most often used between two cats, but it can also be used as a threat for other animals and people.

FACIAL EXPRESSIONS

Cats and humans have very different facial expressions, so it's important not to assign human characteristics to your cat (also known as anthropomorphizing) or you may miss something important. What looks like an adorable, wide-eyed expression of apparent interest on your cat's face could actually be your cat telling you that they're angry.

Since most cats are covered in fur, their facial communication is mainly exhibited through their ears and eyes. We'll explore how small changes in ear, eye, and whisker positioning can mean very different things. Although they express themselves in different ways, cats can still convey excitement, fear, irritation, contentment, trust, and more.

EYES

Cats have excellent night vision, making the colors they're able to see limited and more muted. They are also more nearsighted than typical humans, which means that an object we might see clearly at 100 feet away would appear blurry to your cat. When training, you'll want your cat to have their eyes wide open.

Let's look at some common meanings behind your cat's eye movements:

Narrow pupils: Narrow or slit pupils may indicate arousal by fear, excitement, pleasure, or anger. The size of your cat's pupils will help determine which. Narrow pupils alone can mean excitement when playing with a toy or using catnip. If your cat's ears are back along with narrow pupils, this shows fear.

Dilated pupils: Wide or dilated pupils can mean both fear and excitement, depending on what other signals they're giving. Wide pupils at the vet is likely fear, but the same pupils while playing indicate excitement.

Eyes half-closed: Squinted eyes can signify trust and love, but it can also indicate aggression or discomfort. Look to body language for clues: If your cat is lying down hunched over, their squinted eyes will indicate aggression or perhaps illness. A cat in a relaxed position whose eyes are squinted while you're petting them is exhibiting contentment and trust.

Eyes wide open: A cat whose eyes are open wide shows trust. If your cat's eyes are wide in an unblinking intense stare, however, that's an expression of aggression and intimidation.

Slow blink: A slow blink is another sign of trust. If you slow blink at your cat, you're letting them know you're not a threat. If your cat does this to you, they're letting you know they trust you.

Avoiding eye contact: In natural cat behavior, direct eye contact from one cat to another is seen as assertive and intimidating. If your cat is avoiding direct eye contact, it likely makes them uncomfortable.

EARS

Cats can hear a far wider range of sound frequencies than humans. Their ears are shaped like small satellite antennas, which are helpful to funnel sound. Unlike humans, cats can turn their ears from side to side, allowing them to acutely determine the direction of the sound, which aids in hunting prey. Cat ears are important communication tools, and how they are positioned can indicate a variety of different things. When training, you'll want your cat to have perked ears.

What are your cat's ears trying to tell you?

Perked ears: Upright, forward-facing ears indicate alertness or interest in something. These are also your cat's neutral ear state when they're happy.

Ears flattened back: This means your cat is anxious, nervous, or scared.

Sideways ears: Also known as "airplane ears," this indicates your cat is annoyed, angry, or aggressive. This positioning allows your cat to still hear and be alert while also showing their displeasure.

Twitchy ears: Ears that swivel around express attentiveness, and they're also trying to pick up every bit of sound. This is a handy cat maneuver while hunting or keeping a lookout for danger.

WHISKERS

Whiskers are your cat's sensory equipment. Whisker follicles are three times deeper than regular fur follicles, and they connect to the cat's nervous system. Since cats are nearsighted, whiskers help your cat "see" items up close by sensing even the slightest movement. Their whiskers also help them detect the tiniest changes in air temperature, pressure, and wind. This aids them in navigating their environment at night. And guess what? Cats have 24 whiskers on their muzzle (nose), but they also have numerous other smaller ones on their ears, legs, jaw, and above their eyes.

Whiskers are also used as a form of communication. When training, you'll want your cat to have relaxed whiskers.

Let's translate what your cat's whisker position means:

Relaxed whiskers: The default position of your cat's whiskers is straight out to the sides. This cat is happy and content.

Pulled back: When your cat's whiskers are back against their face, it means they're afraid or stressed.

Pulled forward: Forward-facing whiskers are used when hunting. Cats can sense the slightest change in airflow caused by movement of their prey.

How You Communicate with Your Cat

Do you ever talk to your cat? Although cats can't understand every word coming out of your mouth, they can be trained to understand certain words, tone, and body language. Even if you repeat the same word (such as your cat's name), your cat will react differently depending on whether you say it happily or sternly. The goal of positive reinforcement training is to keep our communication positive, so they have the best experience possible. For best success when training, here are some helpful "Dos" and "Don'ts" for communicating with your feline friend.

DOs

To positively communicate with your cat:

Be a good "listener." We've explored the various ways cats communicate (page 14). Use this information to put your "listening" skills into action.

Use the same words. When training a behavior, you'll use a word or hand signal as the cue for that behavior. Using multiple words or hand gestures for the same cue can be confusing to your cat. For example, if you want to teach your cat to high-five, say "high five" consistently instead of sometimes asking for a "fist bump" or a "boop."

Be consistent. Commit to training at least once a day. If there is too much time between training sessions, your cat may forget the lesson, or they may not pick things up as quickly. Consistency is important during the training session as well. If you've trained your cat to stay on their mat, make sure you don't start accepting looser criteria for that behavior over time.

Stay calm. Training your cat should be fun! If your cat is struggling with training, consider what really might be going on. If you were huffing, saying "no," or showing agitation, they will pick up on that. Your calm demeanor will help prevent your cat from getting stressed.

Keep your body language neutral. Even though cat body language differs from humans' (page 14), your cat already knows what you look like when you're angry or irritated. Sit or stand calmly when training your cat, instead of, for instance, with your arms crossed or hands in your pockets.

DON'Ts

Avoid these communication tactics with your cat, as they may make your cat afraid of you and unwilling to participate in training:

Don't yell. Loud noises can frighten cats. If your cat isn't doing what you want them to do, yelling is not the answer. Yelling is considered aggressive, and your cat will probably run and hide.

Don't greet them aggressively. Pet names or nicknames are fine, but calling your cat something mean (even if meant affectionately) isn't a helpful way to communicate. These names actually reinforce the limiting belief the trainer has of the cat.

Don't threaten your cat. Clapping your hands at your cat, hissing at them, or making threatening motions will make your cat fear you. You want your cat to be comfortable coming close to you and to trust you during training. These gestures hinder that.

Don't punish your cat. Punishing a cat is never okay, nor is it helpful. This includes spraying them with water or rubbing their nose into a mess they made. Positive reinforcement training is about rewarding good behavior and setting your cat up for success.

Don't say "no." Have you ever tried saying "no" in a neutral tone? It's difficult and usually comes across as harsh. Instead of saying "no" in training sessions, ignore the unwanted behavior and reward the behavior you are trying to teach them. Alternately, ask your cat to do a different behavior that can be rewarded. If your cat is scratching furniture, pick them up and place them on the scratcher instead. Anytime you see your cat using the scratcher, give them praise.

KITTY FAQ: "DOES MY CAT KNOW THEIR NAME?"

If you've been using the same name when referring to your cat, they probably know their name by now. But that doesn't mean they're always going to respond to it. Even if a cat knows their name, they're less likely to react when it's spoken by someone they don't like or know well.

People who have punished their cats, or have not interacted with them much, are more likely to have cats that won't respond to their name. That's why positive reinforcement training is so great. Your cat will begin to associate you with delicious food and fun training. Once you're training consistently, your cat will start getting excited when you mention their name. (More on this in chapter 4.)

CHAPTER 3

THE FUNDAMENTALS OF CLICKER TRAINING

In this chapter, we'll walk through everything you need to know about clicker training your cat, including how clicker training works, its benefits, and what you need to get started. You'll be a whiz in no time!

The Clicker and the Cat

Clicker training a cat is very similar to training a dog. But, unlike dogs, cats usually don't follow you around the house, loyally waiting for you to interact with them. Cats are more independent, so the way you train them should be adjusted to suit their personality.

With positive reinforcement training, it's not about dominance, giving orders, or making your cat comply. Think about training as more of a conversation, where you're communicating directly with your cat and building a relationship. With clicker training, you're "clicking" for the desired behavior and rewarding your cat with treats or small bits of food.

Clicker training is based on operant conditioning work, which provides rewards in order to increase desired behaviors and punishment to decrease negative behaviors. From there, clicker training was built around an area of science called *positive reinforcement*, which actively avoids punishing the animal and instead rewards good behavior. Positive reinforcement training was found to be an effective way to train marine mammals because dolphins would simply swim away if they thought they would be punished. By removing fear of punishment, the animals willingly came over to participate and ended up learning much faster.

Clicker training provides clear communication for your cat as to what behaviors you want to see. A "click" on its own is meaningless, but with training, your cat will begin to understand that a click means they did what you wanted and will now get a reward. As you follow the training exercises in part 2, you'll go through the individual steps for teaching each behavior. By keeping the steps small, you can progress to more complex behaviors without it overwhelming you or your cat.

As the trainer, you may need to make slight adjustments based on your cat's unique personality and how they respond. For example, getting your cat to jump over a broomstick isn't going to begin with the broomstick in the air. You'll place it on the ground and work on getting your cat to walk over it first. Then you'll raise the broomstick inch by inch as your cat builds more confidence climbing over it. As the broomstick continues to rise, eventually your cat will have to jump over it. Then, this behavior will be paired with a verbal cue or hand signal. Once your cat performs the behavior on cue consistently, your cat has completed learning the behavior.

Throughout the trainings in part 2, there are some behaviors your cat will be trained to do on cue and others where no cue will be necessary. A *cued behavior* is one where you give the command and the behavior is performed, like "sit." *Uncued behaviors* include behaviors that get your cat comfortable with their surroundings, like coaxing your cat from under the bed.

In both instances, you'll use a clicker to teach the steps for each behavior. The difference lies in the end goal. For instance, the end goal for a cued behavior like "sit" is your cat sitting when you ask them to. When training your cat to come out from under the bed, the end goal is for your cat to not fear you and to be more comfortable in that room. You're simply working with your cat to rid them of their fear. Therefore, this skill doesn't require any command or cue.

However, training isn't completely linear. If your cat jumps over the broomstick one day but won't the next, don't worry. Move back a step and lower the broomstick again to build back your cat's confidence. It's always okay to review the basics or go back a step or two to refresh your cat's memory.

You may also discover your cat requires a different approach to training. If your cat is afraid of the broomstick or spooks themselves after accidentally knocking it over, you may have to go back and get your cat used to it again. This is all normal in training. A good trainer will read their cat's behavior and train at a comfortable pace for the cat.

THE BENEFITS OF CLICKER TRAINING

While there are a lot of benefits of clicker training, it does have its challenges. If your pet isn't driven by food, you'll need to find a different reward, perhaps toys or praise. Also, it takes some practice to get the clicker timing right, so you don't click for the wrong behaviors. We'll work on practicing using your clicker ahead of time.

Now let's jump into the many benefits of clicker training.

IT'S EASY FOR BEGINNERS

Clicker training is easy for beginners to learn; in fact, the entire family can learn it together. This can be especially helpful when you're trying to teach a cat to change an unwanted behavior, such as biting hands. When everyone's on board, the cat receives a consistent message. And all you need to get started is a clicking device, some treats, and, of course, a cat.

IT PRECISELY IDENTIFIES DESIRABLE BEHAVIORS

When you click the clicker, it's like you're taking a snapshot in time. Ideally, at the exact moment you sound the click, the desired behavior is performed. This precision is excellent for a fast-moving cat. You can use a clicker to capture a unique behavior that would otherwise be difficult to train. When done right, your cat has a clear message about what you're asking them to do more of. This is particularly useful in training because you can more easily isolate parts of a complex behavior.

IT HELPS THE CAT FEEL IN CONTROL

Clicker training won't work if your cat doesn't want to participate. Cats are inherently independent, so training may take a little more coaxing for some cats. Training is a two-way street, and you need your cat to be on board. Unlike correction-based methods (or punishment-based training), with clicker training, your cat is choosing to perform the behavior you're asking them to. If they don't feel like training one day or doing a certain behavior, they don't have to. No one will force them to train, which gives your cat more of the autonomy they desire.

IT FORTIFIES THE BOND BETWEEN CAT AND OWNER

Clicker training should be a positive process between you and your cat. Think of each training session like a one-on-one meeting with your cat—it should be fun. During the session, you're giving your cat treats and praise, which strengthens your bond and makes them want to be around you.

As your bond grows and your cat begins to trust you, you're likely to see your cat interact with you more outside of training sessions. They will be more friendly and well-behaved overall. Even timid cats gain confidence after they've started training.

And training doesn't always have to be purposeful. It can just be for fun. I once trained a black bear to ring a hanging cowbell. Whenever I said "We need more cowbell," she'd ring the bell (throwback to the Will Ferrell SNL skit).

IT SAVES TIME AND ENERGY

Clicker training doesn't require long training sessions. You can have a well-trained cat in as little as 15 minutes a day. In fact, short, positive training sessions keep your cat interested and wanting more. It's even better if you can do multiple 3-minute sessions rather than one long 10-minute session. The shorter, the better.

You can train in short bursts when it's convenient for you and when your cat is hungry. Even if you're short on time, most people can find two minutes to train right before feeding their cat their normal meals.

KITTY FAQ: "HOW DO I USE THE CLICKER IN A MULTI-CAT HOUSEHOLD?"

Training in a multi-cat household is possible, but it's more complicated. (We'll walk through a more in-depth training for multiple cats at once on page 58.)

If you have multiple cats at home, I recommend training each cat individually, beginning with the first seven skills in chapter 4. This will give each cat the foundational knowledge and behaviors they'll need to have a successful multi-cat training session. This is especially important if you are new to training.

Find an area that your other cats can't get to, a place where the cat you're training feels comfortable, like a bedroom with the door closed. Alternatively, you can put the other cats away in another room with toys to occupy themselves.

When you transition to multi-cat sessions, if you have three or more cats, start out by training only two cats at once. During each session, you can switch which cats are paired together, but it takes a talented and experienced trainer to train three or more animals at the same time. Even after you graduate to multi-cat sessions, I still recommend individual sessions when training a new behavior with your cat so you avoid distractions and can give them your full attention.

Getting Started

It takes just a few items to get started with clicker training. The basics include a clicker and treats. It's also helpful to have a retractable target wand for pointing, but you can use anything as a target stick provided that it's unique and only used during training. Check out the Resources section on page 105 for recommendations on the best training supplies and where to buy them.

THE CLICKER

A training clicker is a small device that fits in the palm of your hand. It has a button that, when pressed, makes a consistent "click" sound. Most pet stores carry clickers in the dog training section. Any clicker will do, as they are relatively the same for each species.

Clickers come in various shapes and sizes, so find one that fits best in your hand. I recommend one with a wrist lanyard attachment, which will prevent you from dropping it during a session.

Once you have a clicker, it should only be used during training and not as a noisemaker at any other time, so your cat doesn't confuse its meaning.

THE TREATS

This is your cat's favorite part! Clicker training requires a reward that your cat is excited about. For young kittens, their reward can be their regular food, since they have special nutrition requirements. But as your cat gets older, they may not be as excited about their normal food, so treats make a better reward, especially when starting out.

When choosing a training treat, here are a few things to consider:

🐾 Treats should be small (about the size of a pea) so they can be eaten quickly.

🐾 Aim for healthy treats, like dehydrated or freeze-dried chicken bits. Packaged treats tend to be highly processed and higher in calories but are fine in moderation.

🐾 Treats should be high value, meaning good enough that your cat will want to work for them. To keep them interested, only give these special treats during a training session.

🐾 If your cat has health issues, stick with the treats your vet recommends, as some treats may be too high in fats or protein.

For a short 3- to 5-minute training session, you'll need an average of 15 to 20 treats. It's recommended that treats make up no more than 10 percent of your cat's daily calories. If you plan on training multiple times a day, I encourage using a sample-size bag of cat food as treats, so your cat is getting nutritionally complete food, but it's still unique enough flavor-wise that they're willing to work for it. Finally, to ensure you aren't overfeeding your cat, subtract what you give your cat during training from their overall daily food amount.

EVERYTHING ELSE

A clicker and treats are all you really need to get started; however, a few other useful items will help with training as you progress through the book:

☐ Baby gate with mesh front

☐ Cat brush

☐ Cat grass

☐ Catnip bubbles

☐ Cat-safe harness

☐ Cat-safe toothpaste

☐ Cat toys

☐ Cat tree or cat tower

☐ Cat tunnel

☐ Cornstarch

☐ Ear cleaning cloths or cotton balls

☐ Ear cleaning solution

☐ Electric heating pad

☐ Empty eyedrop bottle or your cat's eyedrops

☐ Extendable training stick

☐ Feather toy on stick

☐ Food pouch

☐ Hula hoop

☐ Hurdle or broomstick on top of shoeboxes

☐ Laser pointer

☐ Litter box

- ☐ Mat for each cat (can be a bed, placemat, etc.)
- ☐ Nail clippers
- ☐ Nylon leash
- ☐ Pat bell or call bell
- ☐ Piano (toy or full-size)
- ☐ Scratching post
- ☐ Small opaque plastic cups or walnut shells
- ☐ Soft toothbrush
- ☐ Stools or chairs
- ☐ Transport carrier
- ☐ Weave poles or cones

Clicker Practice

Before you introduce clicker training, it's necessary to practice using the clicker. And after just a few sessions, you'll see your clicking accuracy improve.

Animals are unpredictable, so you'll want to be observant and ready for anything. Practicing with a clicker allows you to get the precise timing down. If you've never used a clicker before, you may not be used to how it feels in your hand. You will also have to coordinate the actions of paying close attention to your cat and having your hand click the clicker at the exact right moment.

DURATION 5 minutes for three sessions, or until or your clicking is precise

MATERIALS

☙ Clicker

☙ TV or YouTube channel with basketball game on

1. Turn on a game of basketball.

2. With the clicker in your dominant hand, every time the basketball touches the court floor, click the clicker.

3. Follow the pace of the game as it changes, clicking more quickly to keep up during intense activity, and work to sync your click with the bouncing of the ball.

4. Continue practicing your clicking until you're able to click as soon as the basketball touches the court floor, without any lag.

PRO TIP

If you don't have a clicker handy, clicking with your tongue can be used in a pinch. It's less precise than a mechanical clicker but works for those times when you don't have a clicker nearby.

Once you feel confident with your skills, you can move on to your first training session with your cat on the next page!

Your First Clicker Training Session: Charging Up the Clicker

The purpose of this exercise is to pair the sound the clicker makes with a reward. This is referred to as "charging up the clicker," because you're taking a meaningless noise and giving it meaning to your cat. To make sure your cat understands, wait at least two hours and then repeat this session before moving on to train actual behaviors.

This exercise should only need to be done twice. Most cats understand after about five or six clicks, but you can keep going until you use 10 to 15 treats.

DURATION 3 minutes for two sessions, or until your cat masters step 6

MATERIALS

🐾 Clicker

🐾 Your cat's favorite treats

1. Find a room where your cat feels most comfortable and won't be distracted.

2. Sit on the ground with your training treats in a container that your cat can't get into.

3. Hold the clicker in your preferred hand and press the button once.

4. Immediately toss a treat to your cat regardless of whether they are looking at you.

5. Once your cat has finished eating, repeat the process of clicking and treating a few times.

6. Sound pairing is complete when your cat looks at you with excitement after they hear the click.

PRO TIP

If your cat is afraid of the clicker sound, try muffling it by wrapping it in a washcloth or clicking while it's in your pocket. Try out different brands of clickers and see what works best for your cat. If your cat is afraid of all clicking noises, see the Resources section (page 105) for a link to an adjustable training whistle that will make the sound softer. You'd blow it in a quick, short burst, just like the clicker.

Clicker Training in 15 Minutes a Day

Now that you've practiced using the clicker, it's time to start training your cat skills and tricks! As a reminder, start with the first seven skills in chapter 4 to build a strong foundation with your cat. Many of those behaviors are used in training more advanced or complex tricks. My advice is to start slow, keep it fun, and go at the pace of your cat. Some cats need more time in the beginning to get the hang of this new experience.

I've found that having a few short training sessions produces much better outcomes than one long session. The 15 minutes a day this book recommends can be broken up into whatever fits your schedule. You might consider three 5-minute sessions, or even five 3-minute sessions. Just keep the first few sessions to 5 minutes or less.

There really is no minimum length of time that a training session needs to be. If your cat is skittish or doesn't seem interested in training at first, each session could be one "click and treat" broken down into 10 mini sessions throughout the day.

FAMILIAR HURDLES

You may encounter some hurdles when training your cat, but don't worry—there are ways around them.

Some of the more common hurdles that cat owners face during training are forgetting where they left off in the last session and not having a plan before starting training. This is why I recommend keeping a training log for each cat. The table on the following page is an example of a simple training log you can fill out after each session. You'll also find a link to a printable training planner in the Resources section (page 105).

You can keep track of your training sessions in a notebook or a computer doc, whatever your preference. You'll want to keep track of:

- The date, to track any patterns and adjust training if necessary

- The time of your session, including how long it was, to ensure sessions aren't too lengthy

- The specific behaviors you worked on, so you don't forget what's next

- Any notes or details about what happened during the session

In addition to keeping you organized, this log can serve as an insight into the patterns and behaviors of your cat, as you may find some cats do better with certain behaviors or during different times of the day.

DATE	TIME/ LENGTH	BEHAVIORS PRACTICED	NOTES
Monday, 11/1	8:30 a.m. 3 minutes	Sit, target	Coco touched her nose to the target today. Started adding in hand cue for "sit."
Monday, 11/1	12 p.m. 5 minutes	Sit, target	Coco is now touching her nose to the target whenever it's presented. Hand cue successfully paired with "sit."

Another hurdle many trainers face is pushing too hard or fast in a session. It's better to end on a good note rather than try to get your cat to repeat a behavior. If, at the beginning of a session, your cat doesn't seem interested, it's okay to practice one or two easy behaviors and then end the session. Try again later when both of you are refreshed.

CLICKER COMMANDMENTS

Okay, you've got the clicker and you've practiced using it. But for success during actual training, you'll want to keep the following "commandments" in mind:

Be consistent. Repetition makes a behavior progress and then stick. Commit to at least one training session with your cat every day.

Ensure the treats are rewarding. Sometimes a cat's lack of progress in training can be as simple as they didn't think the reward was worth doing what you asked of them. Their excitement about the training treat will help them learn the behavior. Test different types of treats to find one that your cat really loves.

Go at your cat's pace. It can be tempting to try to push your cat to the next step, but it can backfire if they aren't ready. Instead, take small incremental steps, so your cat feels comfortable and confident.

Keep your relationship positive. Anyone who occasionally punishes their cat will have to let go of this habit for clicker training to work, even outside of training sessions. Daily interactions influence the cat-owner relationship. If they run away from you outside of a training session because you squirt them with a spray bottle, they surely won't want to come over to you for training. Your entire relationship with your cat matters and will influence your training success.

PART 2

Time to Train

You now have the exciting opportunity to put into practice everything you've learned from part 1. Soon, you'll be able to clicker train your way through the steps of each behavior. The exercises in the coming chapters are arranged from easiest to the most difficult, except for chapter 5, which covers specific behavioral problems that don't necessarily apply to every cat. Ready to get started? Let's go!

CHAPTER 4
PRACTICAL SKILLS

This chapter will cover a series of practical skills that serve as a starting point for training. The first seven are the most important: targeting, name recognition, stationing on a mat, lie down, sit, come, and stay. I recommend teaching these skills to your cat in the order they are presented in this chapter for best success. They will all come in handy, especially in chapters 6 and 7.

Targeting

Teaching your cat to "target," or touch their nose to a target stick, is an important first lesson, as you'll see this trick mentioned throughout the book. Anything can be used as a target stick. Just make sure it's something you only use during training. Retractable click sticks or a stick with a small ball at the end are good options, but something like a ruler or a spatula could work, too.

DURATION	5 minutes, twice a day until trained

MATERIALS

🐾 Target stick

🐾 Clicker

🐾 Your cat's favorite treats

1. Bring your cat into a room where they feel comfortable and won't be distracted.

2. Hold the end of the target stick in front of you, at your cat's eye level. Wait for them to come explore the stick. Once their nose touches the end, click and then immediately reward them with a treat.

3. If your cat doesn't come over to sniff the stick, gently move the target closer to their face. When your cat sniffs the target and touches their nose to it, click and then treat.

4. Continue holding the target at your cat's eye level. Slowly move the stick an inch in any direction. Click and treat when your cat touches their nose to the target.

5. Slowly increase the distance between your cat and the target. The behavior is considered trained when your cat follows you and touches their nose to the target whenever it is presented.

PRO TIP

If your cat isn't touching their nose to the target, rub a treat on the end so the smell will be on the target. Your cat will likely come over to sniff it and touch their nose to it.

Name Recognition

The goal of this skill is to have your cat look at you attentively when you say their name. This response is useful in training sessions if your cat is distracted and you need them to refocus their attention back to you.

DURATION   5 minutes, two or three times a day until trained

MATERIALS

🐾 Clicker

🐾 Your cat's favorite treats

1. Sit with your cat in a room free of distractions.

2. When your cat is looking at you attentively, click and then immediately reward them with a treat.

3. If your cat isn't looking at you, wait until they do, then click and treat.

4. If they're still looking at you attentively, say your cat's name, then click and treat. Repeat this step four or five times.

5. Now, wait until your cat looks away and then say their name. Once they look at you, click and treat. Repeat this step until your cat looks at you every time you say their name.

PRO TIP

If your cat doesn't look away from you during step 5, try introducing a distraction to get them to glance away. For example, you could toss an article of clothing in another direction or throw a pillow toward a corner to distract them.

Station Your Cat on a Mat

This skill teaches your cat to walk to a specific location when asked, and to stay there and wait patiently for the next command. This is useful, for instance, if your cat tends to dart outside whenever you open the door, as you'll be able to direct them to their mat instead. Placing your cat's mat in various locations and having them "station," or move to the various spots, is good physical exercise for them, as well.

Stationing is also useful for training multiple cats at once, as each cat will stay on their mat to avoid interrupting each other's training. You can use differently shaped felt pieces for multiple cats—I trained a cheetah to recognize a triangle as "his shape," and he learned to ignore all other shapes and seek out the triangle!

DURATION 5 minutes, two or three times a day until trained

MATERIALS

- ❧ Your cat's favorite bed or a mat (such as a placemat, bathmat, etc., as long as your cat's body fits on it)
- ❧ Target stick (see page 42)
- ❧ Clicker
- ❧ Your cat's favorite treats

1. Place your cat's mat in a room free of distractions.

2. Use the target stick to position your cat on the mat. Click and reward them with a treat.

3. Tuck the stick away. All four of your cat's feet should still remain on the mat. If they do, click and treat.

4. If your cat climbs off the mat, use the stick to coax them back. Click and treat when they are completely back on the mat (including legs and feet).

5. Tuck the stick away. All four of your cat's feet should remain on the mat. If your cat is able to stay on the mat, continue to click and treat three or four more times to reinforce the behavior.

6. While your cat is on the mat, begin to add a consistent verbal cue, like "station," "mat," or "bed." Click and treat. Only add the verbal cue once your cat has shown they can

consistently station all feet on the mat. Continue with this verbal cue, click, and treat three or four times.

7. Use the target stick to move your cat off the mat. If they comply, click and treat.

8. Use the stick to coax your cat back onto the mat, click, and treat. Add the verbal cue again while your cat's feet are on the mat. Click and treat.

9. To test whether your cat understands the verbal cue, say the verbal cue to station when they are off the mat. If they position themselves with all four feet on the mat, click and treat. The first time they do this, give them a "jackpot" (see Pro Tip) and end the session.

10. As your cat gains confidence in this skill, start moving their mat to a different location each session.

PRO TIP

A jackpot is a special reward, like a handful of treats or a piece of unsalted roasted chicken. A jackpot should be memorable to your cat (and used sparingly).

Lie Down

The goal of this lesson is to get your cat to lie down in a relaxed position with their belly touching the ground. This is a good behavior for times when you want your cat to settle in their bed instead of coming over when you're cooking or entertaining guests, or if your cat is overly excited about something. It's also a behavior your cat will need to know when training the roll-over skill in chapter 7 (page 94).

DURATION   5 minutes, twice a day until trained

MATERIALS

🐾 Clicker

🐾 Your cat's favorite treats

1. In a room free of distractions, have a treat in your hand and place it under your palm on the ground without letting your cat get it.

2. As your cat tries to obtain the treat, they will likely lie down in the process. When they do, click and then reward them with the treat.

3. Repeat steps 1 and 2 three or four times.

4. Now, repeat steps 1 and 2, but without the treat, and with your hand flat on the ground. Click and treat each time your cat successfully lies down.

5. It's time to add a verbal cue. With your hand flat on the ground, say "down" right before your cat lies down. Click and treat. Repeat this step five to eight times.

6. Ask your cat to lie down with the hand and verbal cues before they've started lying down. Click and treat when they do.

PRO TIP

Give your cat a jackpot (see Pro Tip, page 45) the first time they lie down on cue by themselves to help cement this behavior.

Sit

Sure, cats sit when they feel like it, but with this exercise, your cat will do it on cue. This behavior is essential for getting your cat to stay in one location, or when you're training more than one cat at a time.

DURATION 5 minutes, twice a day until trained

MATERIALS

🐾 Target stick

🐾 Clicker

🐾 Your cat's favorite treats

1. Find a comfortable room that is free of distractions.

2. If your cat knows other behaviors well, like targeting (page 42), ask them to perform two behaviors they know first to get the session started. As they comply, click and reward your cat with a treat to create positive momentum.

3. Next, stay still in front of your cat to see if they'll sit on their own. If your cat sits, click and treat.

4. If your cat doesn't sit on their own after a few seconds, hold a treat in your hand and slowly raise it directly above your cat's head. Your cat's head will follow your treat hand and they will likely sit in the process. Once your cat sits, click and treat.

5. Now, add the verbal cue "sit." If your cat sits on their own without prompting, say "sit" before they actually sit down. Click and treat. Repeat the process until your cat sits when given the verbal cue.

6. If your cat needs prompting, say the word "sit" and then raise your treat hand over the cat's head until they sit. Click and treat.

7. Slowly phase out the use of the treat while limiting the hand motion, until your cat will sit to the verbal cue alone.

PRO TIP

You can also capture your cat sitting by watching them throughout the day. Keep a clicker and treats on you. When your cat sits, click and treat. Then continue with step 5.

Come Here

This skill is helpful in getting your cat to come to you from wherever they are in your home. It can be useful when you aren't sure where your cat is but want them to come over, or more importantly, during an emergency.

DURATION   5 minutes, twice a day until trained

MATERIALS

🐾 Clicker

🐾 Your cat's favorite treats

1. Find a room free of distractions.

2. When your cat comes over to you, give them lots of verbal praise and then click and reward them with a treat. You want your cat to associate coming to you with praise and positivity.

3. Slowly increase the distance your cat needs to walk to come to you. Start with only a few feet at first. If your cat is comfortable, try having someone else pick your cat up and take them to the other side of the room. Have them release your cat when you say the word "come." Click and treat when they come back to you.

4. Eventually, your cat should come when you ask, even when they cannot see you or they're in another room. Click and treat each time. To strengthen the behavior, you can also incorporate household noises like a blender or pots and pans when asking your cat to come. The more distractions you introduce and the farther your cat has to travel to reach you, the larger the reward should be to make it worthwhile.

PRO TIP

Don't use your cat's name to get them to come over. You're likely to use your cat's name in the course of everyday life, so this can confuse them. The "come" recall cue needs to be strong so it can be used in a safety situation. A cue will become background noise to your cat if you use it frequently without rewarding each time.

Stay

Before training this behavior, your cat will need to know how to station on a mat (page 44), lie down (page 46), and sit (page 47). Start by building up the length of time your cat remains in one spot (whether sitting, lying down, etc.), and increase your distance from them while asking them to stay. This skill is useful when you want your cat to stay out of the room while you're doing something.

DURATION   5 minutes, twice a day until trained

MATERIALS

- 🐾 Your cat's mat, if stationing (page 44)
- 🐾 Clicker
- 🐾 Your cat's favorite treats

1. In a room free of distractions, ask your cat to either sit, lie down, or station on their mat.

2. Hold your hand out in front of you with your palm forward, as if you are saying "stop," and say "stay." Hold your hand there for a few seconds. Then click and reward them with a treat.

3. Repeat this step three to five times, gradually increasing the amount of time before treating.

4. Once your cat is comfortable staying for a few seconds, back up a bit. Give your cat the cue to stay, and then move back a few inches. Then return to the original starting point. Click and treat.

5. If your cat moved from their position, use a treat or target stick to lure them back and try again using smaller movements.

6. Continue, increasing the distance each time. Make sure to slowly add in different body movements and distractions like tossing toys. These variations will make it tempting for your cat to leave their spot, so it tests whether they understand this behavior.

PRO TIP

This may be difficult for your cat to learn because they want to engage with you and play. Take each step slowly and expect to have to go back and repeat earlier steps.

Wearing a Kitty Harness

Going for a walk with your cat? You'll be the talk of your neighborhood! Wearing a harness is the first step in getting your cat to walk on a leash so they feel completely comfortable in the harness. To keep kitty safe, choose an escape-proof walking jacket or harness made specifically for cats.

DURATION 5 minutes, twice a day until trained

MATERIALS

- 🐾 Escape-proof cat harness
- 🐾 Clicker
- 🐾 Your cat's favorite treats
- 🐾 Target stick (page 42)

1. Place the harness on the ground in front of you. Whenever your cat positively interacts with the harness, click and reward them with a treat.

2. Hold the harness up and open it. Use the target stick to get your cat to stick their head halfway into the harness. Click and treat.

3. Continue working on getting your cat's head into the harness until they feel comfortable with their head all the way through. Click and treat each time.

4. Next, work on slowly bringing the harness between your cat's legs and buckle it over their back. Click and treat. Go very slowly here so your cat isn't afraid.

5. Once the harness is completely on and buckled, use the target stick to coax your cat to move around, getting them used to moving in the harness. Click and treat.

6. Work up to slowly tightening and adjusting the harness to fit, making sure to click and treat throughout the process.

7. Slowly build up the time your cat wears the harness. Focus on rewarding your cat whenever they're in the harness.

PRO TIP

Each cat harness is different, so you may need to adjust the training to work for your particular harness. The Resources section (page 105) includes information about choosing the right harness for your cat.

Cats Can Leash Walk, Too

Getting your cat to walk on a leash is helpful for bringing them to another location. Cats should not be walked from a neck collar, as it puts too much strain on their neck and they can easily escape. First, get your cat fully comfortable wearing a harness (page 50).

DURATION 5 minutes, twice a day until trained

MATERIALS

- 🐾 Nylon leash, non-retractable
- 🐾 Clicker
- 🐾 Your cat's favorite treats
- 🐾 Escape-proof cat harness
- 🐾 Target stick

1. Place the leash on the ground for your cat to explore. Click and reward them with a treat for any positive interactions with the leash. Then, put on their harness. Use the target stick to coax them into walking around; click and treat for walking without the leash attached.

2. If your cat isn't comfortable with the leash, slowly move it around while clicking and treating, until they're comfortable.

3. Once your cat is walking around with their harness, clip the leash to the harness and then immediately unclip it. Click and treat.

4. Next, clip the leash and leave it dangling for a few seconds before unclipping it. Click and treat.

5. Slowly build up the time the leash is clipped and dangling on the floor while your cat moves around.

6. Continue steps 3 to 5 until you can gently hold the leash.

7. While holding the leash, use the target stick to get your cat to take a few steps forward. Click and treat.

8. Slowly continue until your cat is comfortable walking around your home on a leash.

PRO TIP

Retractable leashes can break easily, and chain leashes are too heavy. Check out the Resources section (page 105) for helpful information on choosing cat leashes.

Brushing Your Cat

Brushing your cat is especially important for long-haired breeds, otherwise their fur can become a tangled mess. Younger cats typically do a good job self-grooming, but older cats may need some help as they become less flexible and can't reach everywhere.

DURATION 5 minutes, twice a day until trained

MATERIALS

- 🐾 Cat brush
- 🐾 Clicker
- 🐾 Your cat's favorite treats

1. Place the cat brush on the floor in front of you. Click and reward your cat with a treat for any positive interaction they have with the brush.

2. Hold the brush up to your cat's head level. If they rub their face on the brush, click and treat. Face rubbing means they are claiming it as their own and putting their scent on the brush.

3. Once your cat is comfortable with the brush, slowly move the brush toward their body.

Click and treat. Gently start brushing your cat's head and neck since those are the least sensitive areas.

4. Work up to making small strokes with the brush on your cat. Click and treat with each brush.

5. Keep brushing in small movements to get your cat used to the feeling. Build up to larger movements before moving to another part of your cat's body.

6. As your cat gets used to each area being brushed, you can move on to the next area. Some cats are more sensitive to brushing than others, so use less pressure starting out.

PRO TIP

Each cat will have a brush they prefer, so it's helpful to have a few styles to test out. For help picking out a brush, see the Resources section (page 105).

Kitty Pedicure

Clipping your cat's nails helps cut down on destructive scratching and snagging on things. Each nail has an area of blood vessels and nerves called a quick that you don't want to cut into, as it will be painful and bleed (see Pro Tip). It looks like a dark line in the middle of your cat's nail.

DURATION   5 minutes, once a day until trained

MATERIALS

- 🐾 Clicker
- 🐾 Your cat's favorite treats
- 🐾 Cat nail clippers
- 🐾 Cornstarch (a small amount)

1. First, get your cat used to you touching their feet and moving their toes around. Choose one foot. Click as you gently touch your cat's foot and give them a treat. Keep the nail clippers visible.

2. Work up to touching your cat's foot longer, picking it up, gently squeezing it, and moving their toes around. Click and treat for each small movement.

3. Once your cat is used to one foot being handled, do the same for the remaining feet.

4. Once they're comfortable with all feet being touched, slowly pick up the clippers and put them down. Move the clippers closer to your cat's foot. Click and treat each time they don't react.

5. Work up to touching the clippers to your cat's foot to touching a nail, all while clicking and treating.

6. Finally, clip the tiniest bit of nail off one toe. Click and treat.

7. Continue clipping tiny bits off your cat's nails while rewarding them. At first, you may only cut a few millimeters from one nail. Repeat this training once a day.

PRO TIP

If you cut the quick, don't beat yourself up. Just apply a glob of cornstarch and pressure to the area until bleeding has stopped.

Sparkling White Kitty Teeth

Brushing your cat's teeth daily is great for maintaining their health, cutting down on expensive dental procedures, and preventing other health and mouth issues for your cat. It's important to only use cat-safe toothpaste and not those intended for humans, as many sweeteners found in them are not safe for pets.

DURATION 5 minutes, twice a day until trained

MATERIALS

- 🐾 Soft pet toothbrush
- 🐾 Cat-safe toothpaste
- 🐾 Clicker
- 🐾 Your cat's favorite treats

1. Put a small dab of kitty toothpaste on the toothbrush bristles.

2. Hold the toothbrush out in your hand with the bristles facing toward your cat. Click and give them a treat for every positive interaction they have, including sniffing, licking, and rubbing their face on it.

3. Once your cat is comfortably licking the toothbrush, gently lift your cat's upper lips and rub the toothbrush on the outer surface of their teeth by their gums. Click and treat. Repeat this until they're comfortable.

4. If your cat doesn't like their lips being moved, click and treat each time they let you move them and slowly increase the length of time spent moving them before you try to brush their teeth.

5. The goal is to be able to gently brush the exterior of your cat's teeth by their gums on both sides of their mouth, top, and bottom. Click and treat as you slowly work up to different parts of their mouth.

PRO TIP

You don't need to brush the interior of your cat's mouth since their tongue helps prevent plaque buildup there. Most cats don't like their mouths being opened wide, either.

Squeaky Clean Ears

Cats are great at cleaning their own ears, but kittens or older cats may need a little extra help. Speak with your vet before starting an ear-cleaning regimen to rule out any possible infection or a ruptured eardrum, and learn how often you should clean your cat's ears.

DURATION 5 minutes, twice a day until trained

MATERIALS

- Squeeze bottle of ear cleaning solution
- Cotton balls
- Clicker
- Your cat's favorite treats

1. For the entire training process, you'll use a capped solution bottle. Place the capped solution bottle and cotton balls on the ground and let your cat investigate them. Click and reward them with a treat for any positive interaction they have with the bottle or cotton balls.

2. Leaving the bottle on the ground, get your cat used to ear touching. Gently touch their ear flap, then click and treat.

3. Slightly pull the ear flap back so the ear area is more exposed. Click and treat. Make sure you aren't folding their ear flap back because most cats find this uncomfortable.

4. While their ear is being held, bring the capped solution bottle to the opening of their ear. Don't put the tip inside your cat's ear, as that could damage their eardrum. Click and treat.

5. Gently rub the base of your cat's ear like you would if solution had been applied. Click and treat.

6. Finally, hold up a cotton ball and touch it to the base of your cat's ear. Click and treat.

PRO TIP

It's easiest to apply ear solution when your cat is somewhat restrained. You can do this when your cat is snuggled in your lap to make it easier to hold them while cleaning their ears. You want them to feel comfortable throughout the training and not associate your lap with being a scary place.

Making Eye Drops Less Scary

Some cats may need eye drops for bacterial infections, cataracts, or other issues. However, this behavior is helpful to train before your cat is prescribed eye drops. This way, if your cat ever needs eye drops, this behavior will already be trained and there will be less stress for you and your cat.

You'll begin training with the eye-drop bottle closed and only work up to the actual eye drops when your cat needs them. You can also ask your veterinarian if they have any non-medicated eye drops that are safe to practice with.

DURATION 5 minutes, twice a day until trained

MATERIALS

☙ An empty eye-drop bottle, or your cat's eye drops

☙ Clicker

☙ Your cat's favorite treats

1. Get your cat to sit comfortably in front of you. Have the eye-drop bottle on the floor in front of you with the cap on. Click and reward them with a treat for any positive interaction they have with the bottle.

2. Lift up the bottle and place it back down on the floor. Click and treat. Repeat this a few times until your cat is comfortable with the bottle moving around.

3. Lift the bottle and move it slowly toward your cat. Click and treat. Slowly move the bottle toward your cat's head and eyes while clicking and treating.

4. With one hand holding the bottle, use the other hand to gently touch the area on either side of your cat's eye, making sure not to directly touch their eye. Click and treat.

5. If you're having trouble holding the clicker while doing this, use your tongue to make a click sound instead. Avoid holding the clicker near your cat's head because it will be very loud to them.

6. Work your way up to holding their eye open briefly and moving the eye-drop bottle over to above their eye. Click and treat. If your cat becomes scared or uneasy, go back a few steps and move forward more slowly.

7. If you have vet-approved practice drops, work up to putting a droplet in one eye. The first time this happens, give them a jackpot (see Pro Tip, page 45) and end the session.

8. Work up to putting the eye drops in both eyes. You can go through the steps focusing on one eye at a time or alternating eyes, depending on your cat's comfort level.

PRO TIP

Most cats do not like being restrained or having their eyes held open. Take very small steps throughout this training so you don't make it scary. This behavior could take weeks or months of consistent training, depending on your cat.

Training Multiple Cats at Once

Before training multiple cats at once, each cat will need to know the first seven behaviors from this chapter, ensuring that each cat understands the foundational behaviors before multiple-cat training begins and before moving on to more difficult skills. Start with two cats and work your way up to more. The more cats you train at once, the more difficult it is.

DURATION 5 minutes, twice a day until trained

MATERIALS

- 🐾 Mats or beds for stationing (page 44)
- 🐾 Clicker
- 🐾 Your cats' favorite treats
- 🐾 Target stick

1. Place each cat's mat in front of you, about two feet apart from one another. One at a time, ask each cat to station. Click and reward them with a treat.

2. Train one cat at a time, alternating back and forth. For the cat you aren't actively training, continue to click and treat for staying on their mat and not interrupting the other cat.

3. If a cat gets off their mat on their own, ask them to station again or use the target stick to lead them back onto the mat. Click and treat.

4. For the cat you're actively training, ask them for behaviors they know, like targeting (page 42), lie down (page 46), or sit (page 47). Click and treat.

5. For each click to the cat you're actively training, also give a treat to the other cat for staying on their mat. This lets the second cat know that staying on their mat is the desired behavior. It also prevents them from stealing the training cat's treats.

PRO TIP

When training new behaviors, train each cat one-on-one. You can use multiple-cat sessions to spice up your training sessions. Some cats perform trained behaviors perfectly in an undistracted room but forget once they're back in the "real world." Having other cats around adds a distraction to test behaviors you've already trained.

CHAPTER 5

SOLVING BEHAVIORAL PROBLEMS

Cats are fun, but sometimes they adopt unwanted behaviors. This chapter will teach you how to train away some of the most common behavioral problems in cats. There's no need to go in order here. Feel free to skip around to the specific problem you're having with your fuzzy feline, and you'll discover just how to correct their behavior.

See, Petting Isn't Too Bad

The key to getting your reluctant cat to agree to petting is to go slowly and "listen" to them. Some cats are sensitive and don't like being petted along their back and would prefer you pet around their head and neck area. Most cats don't want their belly, feet, or tail petted.

DURATION   5 minutes, twice a day until trained

MATERIALS

- 🐾 Clicker
- 🐾 Your cat's favorite treats

1. Hold your hand out toward your cat. Click and reward them with a treat for any positive interaction they have with your hand.

2. Slowly touch the top of your cat's head, gently but firmly. Click and treat.

3. Pet the top of your cat's head in one-second intervals. Click and treat with each pet.

4. Next, after each one-second interval, ask for a different behavior your cat knows, such as targeting or sitting. This will break up the lesson if they're not used to being petted. Click and treat. Then return to step 3, clicking and treating less frequently. Go back and forth between steps 3 and 4 until your cat is used to you briefly touching the top of their head.

5. Increase the length of time your cat allows you to pet them, while also moving your hand down to their neck area as well. Click and treat throughout the intervals.

6. Continue moving to different body parts of your cat, like their back. Click and treat. Watch their behavior, and try not to pet any area that makes your cat feel uncomfortable. Watch for signs like their ears going back, flicking their tail around, or vocalizing at you.

PRO TIP

Most cats can learn to like having their heads and necks petted. It's better not to force the issue with other body parts if they find it overstimulating.

Picking Kitty Up

Training your cat to be more comfortable being picked up is helpful when you need to move them from one location to another, whether it's to another room or to the vet.

DURATION 5 minutes, twice a day until trained

MATERIALS

🐾 Clicker

🐾 Your cat's favorite treats

1. Start by petting your cat on their head and neck. Gently place one hand on your cat's chest between their front legs. Click and reward them with a treat.

2. Place your other hand over your cat's shoulder blades so that you're firmly holding them. Click and treat.

3. Rotate your hands so both are on your cat's chest, a bit away from their armpits. Click and treat.

4. Slowly raise your cat's front legs up one inch. Click and treat. Work your way to raising your cat about one foot off the ground while clicking and rewarding with treats.

5. With one hand on your cat's chest, use your other hand to touch your cat's hind legs and feet. Click and treat.

6. Continue lifting your cat at a low height. Click and treat each time. Work your way up to one hand on your cat's chest area and the second arm supporting their hind end. Ideally, this should be done in a sitting position.

7. Work your way to standing upright, holding your cat in various positions to find how they prefer to be held. Some cats like being held like a baby, upright with their hind legs supported fully, or even draped over your shoulder.

PRO TIP

When picking up your cat, make sure you're lifting at their chest and not their sensitive belly or they might try to bite you.

No More Hiding Under the Bed

Hiding under the bed is a common safety response; cats know it's difficult for people and other animals to get to them. Instead of dragging your cat out from under the bed, this training will encourage your cat to come out on their own. Your cat should know targeting (page 42) before training this skill.

DURATION 5 minutes, twice a day until trained

MATERIALS

* 🐾 Target stick
* 🐾 Clicker
* 🐾 Your cat's favorite treats

1. Wait until your cat is located in their usual hiding spot. Extend the target stick close to where your cat is hiding. If they touch the target, click and reward them with a treat.

2. Move the target one inch away from your cat. When they touch it, click and treat.

3. Continue to move the target stick around in the hiding spot, clicking and treating. This will make your cat more comfortable and likely to follow the target stick out from under the bed.

4. Slowly move the target stick an inch or two outside of the bed, where your cat can stay mostly underneath but still reach the target. Click and treat. The first time your cat ventures out from under the bed, give a jackpot (see Pro Tip, page 45) and end the session.

5. In later sessions, continue to target under and outside the bed, increasing the distance outside the bed inch by inch. Work your way up so your cat comes all the way out from under the bed while clicking and treating.

PRO TIP

If your cat is frightened, keep the sessions short. In the beginning, you can entice them with larger jackpots when they come out from under the bed, like a piece of unsalted turkey or a spoonful of wet food.

No More Destructive Scratching

Cats scratch to keep their nails healthy, mark their territory, and get some stretching in. Sometimes cats choose something we don't want them to scratch, like furniture. With this training, you'll redirect your cat to approved scratching options.

DURATION   5 minutes, twice a day until trained

MATERIALS

- 🐾 Cat scratchers of various materials (cardboard, sisal, carpet, etc.)
- 🐾 Clicker
- 🐾 Your cat's favorite treats
- 🐾 Target stick

1. Take note of where your cat destructively scratches. Notice the materials and the position of their body when scratching.

2. Purchase two or three cat scratchers (per cat) in their preferred scratching materials. Make sure the scratchers are sturdy and allow your cat to scratch in their preferred position. Some cats like scratching horizontally; others prefer vertical posts.

3. Place the scratchers near where your cat is destructively scratching. Click and reward them with a treat for any positive interaction with the scratchers.

4. Use the target stick to coax your cat into climbing on the scratchers. Click and treat.

5. If your cat is hesitant about using a vertical post, place the post on its side. Use the target stick to coax them onto the scratcher. Click and treat for targeting with their feet on the post.

6. Stand the post up once they're more comfortable. Click and treat for targeting with their feet touching the post.

PRO TIP

If needed, sprinkle a small amount of catnip onto the scratchers. This will usually entice the cat to come over and rub on the scratchers. Make sure to replace any scratchers that get old.

Bedtime Kitty Snuggles

If you'd like your cat to snuggle in bed with you but your cat has other ideas, these steps will help encourage your cat to stay with you at night. Cats love warmth, and these steps enlist the help of a heating pad to make your bed an enticing place to be.

DURATION 5 minutes, twice a day until trained

MATERIALS

- 🐾 Clicker
- 🐾 Your cat's favorite treats
- 🐾 Electric heating pad, heated blanket, or hot-water bottle
- 🐾 Target stick

1. If your cat isn't comfortable in your bedroom yet, give them a few days with access to your room. Click and reward them with treats when they follow you into the room.

2. During your bedtime routine, place the heating pad on low in your bed where you'd like your cat to sleep. Click and treat if your cat jumps up onto your bed and lies down.

3. If your cat doesn't jump onto your bed on their own, use the target stick to coax them up. Click and treat for every successful target.

4. Target your cat over to the heating pad so they can investigate it and get comfortable on your bed.

5. Keep clicking and treating as your cat snuggles on your bed while you get in and go to sleep. For safety, turn off and remove the heating pad before going to sleep yourself (see Pro Tip).

6. If you're already in bed, call your cat over and target them up onto the bed with you already in it. Click and treat.

PRO TIP

You can also use your own body warmth to warm up the bed. Entice your cat into bed by making a nest of blankets for them to snuggle in as well.

My Bed, Not Yours

You may be okay with your cat in your bedroom, but there may be times you don't want to share your bed with them. These steps will help keep them away. Multi-level cat trees can be purchased at most pet stores or online.

DURATION   5 minutes, twice a day until trained

MATERIALS

🐾 Cat bed and cat tree

🐾 Target stick

🐾 Clicker

🐾 Your cat's favorite treats

1. Place a cat tree in your room with one of your cat's beds. Cats prefer to sleep up high, so if the tower is higher than your bed (and comfy), you'll have an easier time getting them to sleep there.

2. Use the target stick to coax them into the cat tree bed. Click and reward them with a treat for each successful target.

3. Once your cat is in their bed, use the verbal cue "stay" (page 49). Click and treat for increasing lengths of time they stay in the bed.

4. Anytime you see your cat in your bed, use the target stick to coax them back into their cat tree bed. Click and treat.

5. Before you go to bed, target your cat into their bed for the night. Click and treat.

PRO TIP

If your cat won't stay in the cat tree bed, make sure it's not in the way of a draft or too exposed. Cats like feeling safe while sleeping, so a corner might be a good location for the tower.

No More Counter Surfing

Cats are constantly exploring their surroundings, which may include your kitchen counters and other surfaces. They're attracted to food, smells, running water, and the safety that the height of countertops provides. Once you determine why they're drawn to them, follow these steps to keep them off.

DURATION 5 minutes, twice a day until trained

MATERIALS

- 🐾 Alternative items (optional, see step 2)
- 🐾 Target stick
- 🐾 Clicker
- 🐾 Your cat's favorite treats

1. Watch your cat to see why they're going on your counters in the first place. Are they just sniffing around or sneaking food? Are they in the kitchen sink licking up water droplets? Or do they simply like hanging out up high? Make note of the possibilities.

2. Offer a better option for your cat nearby. If your cat likes flowing water, get a cat water fountain that bubbles. If your cat likes being up high, place cat shelves or a cat tree in a nearby room so they can see what's going on in the kitchen. If your cat is looking for food, offer them puzzle cat toys where they have to work for their food.

3. The next time you see your cat on a countertop, hold the target stick out near the ground. As soon as they jump down, click and reward them with a treat.

4. If your cat runs away before you can hold out the target, toss a treat onto the floor instead. Click as soon as your cat's feet touch the ground and let them eat the treat on the ground.

5. Repeat step 3 or 4 each time your cat is on the countertop. Then, use the target stick to bring your cat over to the alternative option you've provided for them. Click and treat for following the target and using the alternatives.

6. Continue this process until they no longer jump onto your countertops. Persistence by everyone in the household to train this behavior the same way will speed the process. Otherwise, your cat may think that it's only in the presence of certain people that they can't be on the countertop.

PRO TIP

You can speed this process by temporarily cluttering up your countertops so they're too messy and your cat can't get onto them easily. They'll be more likely to use the better options you've set up.

Cat, Meet Other Pets

Whether your cat is new or you're bringing home another cat or dog (or any other animal they might interact with), taking steps to ensure your cat is comfortable during introductions will help prevent fights and behavior issues down the road. This lesson focuses on acclimating a new cat to a home with other pets.

DURATION   5 minutes, twice a day until trained

MATERIALS

- 🐾 Supplies to make your cat comfortable (see step 1)
- 🐾 Clicker
- 🐾 Your cat's favorite treats
- 🐾 Target stick
- 🐾 Mesh front baby gate

1. Start by putting your new cat in a separate room with a solid door so they can't escape. This room should be comfortable with a bed, toys, a perch, scratchers, food, water, and a litter box.

2. Leave your new cat in this room for four or five days so they can get acclimated. Give other household pets access to the other side of the solid door so they can smell one another.

3. Start training your cat wherever they seem comfortable in the room. Eventually begin training closer to the closed door so your cat becomes more comfortable with other pets nearby. Click and reward with a treat for all positive behaviors and interactions.

4. Throughout the first week, swap out a few of the new cat's toys with your other pets' toys to let them get used to their scent.

5. After the fifth day, put your other pets into a closed-off room with a solid door and let the new cat out to explore freely for a few hours, so they can spread their scent and get the lay of the home. Allow your cat full access to their original room in case they get spooked.

6. Repeat this for three or four days. Try training behaviors with the new cat when they're out exploring. Click and treat whenever appropriate.

7. If there aren't any negative noises between your pets through the solid door, put up a mesh-front baby gate on the new cat's door and open the solid door. Stand on the side that allows you to close the door quickly if necessary. If you have multiple pets, only let the calmest one out at this time. Allow them to sniff each other. Don't use the clicker or treats here, since this may cause food aggression between the two. Spend time with both pets and just observe. If they come over to you, give them praise and attention.

8. Alternate which pet is at the gate if you have a multi-pet household. Give your new cat a few hours to rest in between each introduction.

9. Eventually, there will be a point where you can let your pets interact fully with one another. Make sure there aren't any aggressive noises coming from any of the pets and all seem relaxed before doing this.

10. Always give your new cat access to their room for safety and comfort. If you're introducing your cat to dogs, get a baby gate with a small cat hole in it so your cat can escape back into their room. Make sure there are cat towers and high places that only the cat can access.

PRO TIP

Take introductions very slowly, especially if you are introducing your new cat to large dogs. It can take between three and five weeks for your new cat to get acclimated with your other pets. It can still take eight months or longer for cats to develop a friendship with other pets.

Ouch! Stop Biting Hands

Cats will often bite hands because people allowed them to do this as kittens, wiggling their fingers and letting them attack. As a kitten, those bites don't hurt, but as an adult cat, it can become a painful problem. For best success, everyone in your household should be in agreement not to let your cat play with anyone's bare hands, including visitors.

DURATION   5 minutes, twice a day until trained

MATERIALS

🐾 Cat toys

🐾 Clicker

🐾 Your cat's favorite treats

1. Every time you play with your cat, use a toy. Starting out, use a cat toy on a stick to keep your hands farther from their mouth.

2. If your cat attacks your hand when playing, remove your hand and put a toy in front of them. Click and reward them with a treat when they start playing with the toy instead of going after your hand.

3. Continue repeating this process to ensure you never play with your cat using your hands.

PRO TIP

Until this behavior is trained, hold off on trying to pet your cat immediately after playing with them to avoid them instinctively biting your hands.

Shhh! Stop Meowing All the Time

Cats might meow when they're hungry, want to play, or simply want to talk to you. Some cats take this to the extreme and seem to be meowing constantly. The following training will reward your chatty friend for their quiet behavior.

DURATION 5 minutes, twice a day until trained

MATERIALS

🐾 Clicker

🐾 Your cat's favorite treats

1. Try to stop the meowing before it even starts by immediately clicking and treating at the beginning of a session if they're being quiet.

2. If your cat is meowing, wait until they are quiet before you click and treat.

3. Starting out, you'll want to click at even the briefest moment when your cat is not meowing. Then slowly build up the length of time that your cat must be quiet before clicking and giving them a treat.

PRO TIP

It's easiest to train one behavior at a time. If your cat is meowing when you're training a different behavior, it's easiest to get your cat to be quiet first. Then when you start training other behaviors, your cat won't be meowing throughout the training session.

No More Feet Attacks

Cats often attack their human's feet during play. It may be a little maddening, but it's not out of aggression. Through this training, each time they try to go for your feet, you'll redirect your cat's attention to their toys and reward them for focusing on their toys.

DURATION | 5 minutes, twice a day until trained

MATERIALS

🐾 Cat toys

🐾 Clicker

🐾 Your cat's favorite treats

1. Observe the situations in which your cat attacks your feet. Are your feet wiggling under a blanket? Are you walking by the couch while your cat is hiding underneath?

2. The next time you're in a situation where your feet typically get attacked, have some cat toys on hand. Long wand cat toys are good for this purpose.

3. If your cat attacks your feet, use the cat toy to play with them instead. As soon as they play with the cat toy, click and reward them with a treat.

4. Preemptively play with the cat toys away from your feet so your cat doesn't attack. Click and treat when they are playing nicely with you and the toys.

5. Continue these steps until your cat is no longer attacking feet and instead goes for their toys as a first choice.

PRO TIP

To avoid confusing the cat, make sure all family members are in agreement not to encourage your cat to attack any feet.

Crate Training

Crate training is useful for transporting your cat. Training your cat to go in and out of their crate voluntarily will reduce stress for everyone, especially in an emergency.

DURATION 5 minutes, twice a day until trained

MATERIALS

- 🐾 Cat crate
- 🐾 Clicker
- 🐾 Your cat's favorite treats
- 🐾 Target stick

1. Place the crate on the ground with the door open (but secured) or off. Click and reward with a treat if your cat walks toward the crate.

2. Toss a treat into the crate. As soon as your cat sticks their head inside, click and let them eat the treat. Continue until your cat goes fully inside the crate.

3. If your cat doesn't go all the way inside, use a target stick to coax them in.

4. Once they're comfortable going in and out, put the door back on. Target your cat in and out with the door open. Click and treat.

5. When your cat is inside the crate, close the door an inch and then open again. Continue slowly, increasing the movement of the door until it's closed but not latched. Click and treat.

6. Build up to latching the crate and increasing the time it stays closed. Click and treat.

7. With the door latched, raise the crate one inch off the ground and put it back down. Click and treat. Open the crate door once it's back on the ground so your cat can exit. Ask your cat to return to the crate, latch it, and raise it again.

8. Increase the distance your cat is raised. Work up to walking around with your cat in the crate. Click and reward for each step.

PRO TIP

Leave the opened crate out all the time, with their bed inside, so your cat gets used to the crate.

Chewing Challenge

Cats like to chew on things like cords, plastic, plants, and more, often because they are bored or curious. The easiest solution is to hide those items, but you can also train your cat to stop chewing on things they shouldn't be.

DURATION 5 minutes, twice a day until trained

MATERIALS

- 🐾 Puzzle feeder bowls/toys and cat toys
- 🐾 Clicker
- 🐾 Your cat's favorite treats

1. Observe when your cat is chewing (and on what) to determine whether it's around their feeding time or if they seem bored.

2. If your cat is chewing around dinnertime, it's likely due to hunger. You can solve this by making sure your cat is eating enough food. One way to make food last longer is to put their food in puzzle feeder bowls and toys.

3. If you find your cat is chewing due to boredom or if they want to play, get a variety of cat toys that are crinkly and have different textures similar to what they're chewing on.

4. The next time your cat is chewing something they shouldn't, get their attention by tossing a toy in their direction. Click and reward them with a treat if they start playing with the toy instead.

5. When your cat starts heading to the thing you don't want them to chew, toss them a toy and play with them. Click and treat.

6. Continue this process until they start going to their toys to chew, instead of to the objects they shouldn't be chewing.

PRO TIP

Puzzle feeders are one of the best ways to keep your cat from destructively chewing since it engages your cat's mind and takes longer for them to access the food. Check out the Resources section (page 105) for some puzzle feeder recommendations.

Don't Jump On Me!

Cats love being up high, and humans can sometimes appear to be nice tall "trees" for a furry friend to climb. But their claws can be painful! Have no fear—this prickly behavior can be curbed in a few short steps. With this training, the cat tree becomes a more fun and positive choice for them.

DURATION   5 minutes, twice a day until trained

MATERIALS

- 🐾 Cat trees
- 🐾 Target stick
- 🐾 Clicker
- 🐾 Your cat's favorite treats

1. Make sure your cat has cat trees or towers and other places to climb high so you aren't their only option.

2. Whenever your cat looks like they're going to climb up or jump on you, use the target stick to coax them away from you by having them follow the target instead. Click and reward them with a treat.

3. If your cat does jump on you, remove them and place them onto their cat tree. Target them around on the cat tree, clicking and treating as they move around.

4. Make an agreement that no one in the household will allow your cat to climb or jump on them, even as a tiny kitten; otherwise, this will be confusing and result in bad habits later on.

PRO TIP

If your cat has a favorite spot they jump on you from, like the back of the couch, outwit them by putting items in that spot, blocking them from using it.

CHAPTER 6

FUN GAMES

Ready for some fun? This chapter is all about games, training your cat to have fun with you, and providing connection through play. Cats love to hunt and are naturally curious creatures. In addition to being fun, these games keep their minds active.

Follow the Dot

Laser pointers are such fun toys to use, especially with your cat, and can be found at most pet stores. These can also be used as a target to get your cat to move to a new location. Make sure to never shine the laser into your cat's eyes or let your cat look directly into the laser, as this will damage their eyesight.

DURATION   5 minutes, twice a day until trained

MATERIALS

🐾 Laser pointer

🐾 Clicker

🐾 Your cat's favorite treats

1. Shine the laser pointer onto the ground directly in front of your cat. As soon as they paw at the red laser dot, click and reward them with a treat.

2. If your cat isn't pawing at the dot, wiggle the laser slightly to make the dot move. Click and treat as soon as your cat paws the dot.

3. Start moving the dot a few inches away. When your cat paws the dot, click and treat.

4. Keep moving the laser dot farther away and to different locations around the room. Each time they successfully paw the red dot, click and treat.

PRO TIP

A laser pointer can also be used as a target when you want your cat to go somewhere your regular target stick can't reach.

Catch That Prey!

Teaching your cat how to chase prey may come naturally, but some domesticated cats never seem to get the hang of it. With this behavior, you'll witness your cat's natural predatory ability and build up their confidence by letting them successfully "catch prey."

DURATION   5 minutes, twice a day until trained

MATERIALS

🐾 Mouse or feather toy, on a string

🐾 Clicker

🐾 Your cat's favorite treats

1. Tie a mouse or feather toy to a string or shoelace so the toy mimics a prey item. Hold the end of the string and lay the toy on the ground. If your cat goes over to explore the toy, click and reward them with a treat.

2. Wiggle the mouse toy. Click and treat when your cat interacts with it.

3. Continue to wiggle and move the mouse toy, increasing its distance from your cat. Click and treat whenever your cat engages with the toy.

4. Toss the mouse toy a few feet away from your cat. Click and treat when your cat chases the toy.

5. Eventually you'll be able to wiggle the toy and toss it with your cat without a reward or treat. Your cat will consider it a reward in itself just to play and chase their prey.

PRO TIP

If your cat doesn't take to the toy you're using, find a toy that uses real fur or feathers. Cats have a high prey drive, so they should take to chasing prey fairly quickly if it incorporates the "real deal."

Ring the Bell

This unique trick can be utilized to alert you to something, perform a musical routine, or just have fun with your cat. This lesson uses a call bell, but you can train using any kind of bell.

DURATION   5 minutes, twice a day until trained

MATERIALS

- 🐾 Pat bell or call bell
- 🐾 Clicker
- 🐾 Your cat's favorite treats

1. Place the bell on the floor between you and your cat. Position your hand out in front of your cat, directly over the bell, with your palm facing up. Click and reward them with a treat for any movement of your cat's paw.

2. If your cat won't move, move your hand closer to their front foot. Wiggle your fingers a bit. Click and treat if they move their paw toward your hand.

3. Put your hand back out with your palm facing up. Click and treat for any movement of your cat's paw toward your hand.

4. The first time your cat touches their paw to the palm of your hand, give them a jackpot (see Pro Tip, page 45).

5. Move your hand away from the bell, or have your fingers slowly spread open so when your cat puts their paw in your hand, they touch the bell. Click and treat.

6. Slowly move toward replacing your hand with the bell, so the cat's paw is touching the bell. Work toward just pointing at the bell. Whenever you point to the bell, your cat's paw should touch the bell, instead of your hand. Click and treat.

7. Once your cat is reliably ringing the bell with your hand cue, say "bell" immediately before giving the hand cue. Click and treat each time your cat rings the bell with the verbal cue.

PRO TIP

Use your pointed finger as a cue, or fade that out to only use the verbal cue.

Fetch!

Yes, cats can be taught to fetch, just like dogs! The key is to use their favorite type of toy. Some cats prefer ball toys, while others may prefer mouse toys. Use whatever type of toy your cat loves and would be interested in for this training. If you've already trained the Come Here behavior (page 48), this will make step 3 easier.

DURATION 5 minutes, twice a day until trained

MATERIALS

- 🐾 Ball or mouse toy
- 🐾 Clicker
- 🐾 Your cat's favorite treats

1. Grab your cat's favorite toy and roll it a few feet away from them. As soon as your cat picks up the toy in their mouth, click and reward them with a treat.

2. Do this four or five times until your cat understands you want them to pick up the toy.

3. Whenever your cat picks up the toy in their mouth, call them over to you. Click and treat.

4. Each time your cat picks up the toy, call your cat back to you until they're reliably bringing the toy to you on command.

5. The next time you toss the toy, say the word "fetch." Your cat should go get the toy and bring it back. Reward your cat with a jackpot (see Pro Tip, page 45) the first time they fetch the toy on cue.

6. Once you start incorporating the word "fetch," you'll want to stop using the word "come" so it doesn't confuse the cues.

PRO TIP

If your cat won't pick up the toy in their mouth at the beginning, rub a treat on the toy to get the scent of food on it.

Popping Bubbles

Everyone loves playing with bubbles, but have you ever blown bubbles for your cat to pop? If not, wait until you try this. It'll be as much fun for you to watch as for them to do! As your cat gains confidence popping, they're more likely to jump or leap to pop the bubbles. Make sure the bubbles are nontoxic, as your cat may ingest some bubble liquid in the process of popping. There are even catnip-infused bubbles you can buy to keep your cat engaged!

DURATION 5 minutes, twice a day until trained

MATERIALS

- 🐾 Nontoxic bubbles and bubble wand
- 🐾 Clicker
- 🐾 Your cat's favorite treats

1. With your cat in front of you, blow a small bubble so it's still attached to the bubble wand. Hold the wand in front of your cat. Click and treat for any interaction that pops the bubble.

2. Repeat step 1 four or five times until your cat begins to understand the concept of popping the bubble. Make sure you're clicking at the exact moment the bubble is being popped and not when your cat touches the wand.

3. Next, blow one bubble into the air. Click and treat for any motion your cat makes to pop the bubble, even if they miss.

4. Continue this until your cat reliably pops any bubbles you blow.

PRO TIP

If your cat won't pop a floating bubble, teach your cat the high-five behavior first (page 97) so they learn to pop the bubble while giving you a high five.

Tunnel Run

Teaching your cat how to run through a tunnel can be great exercise. You could even use this as part of a kitty agility course in your house and train your own personal ninja warrior cat! Cats especially love tunnels because it gives them a place to hide and pounce out from.

DURATION   5 minutes, twice a day until trained

MATERIALS

- 🐾 Cat tunnel
- 🐾 Clicker
- 🐾 Your cat's favorite treats
- 🐾 Target stick

1. Place the cat tunnel near you. Let your cat explore the tunnel on their own to get comfortable. Click and reward them with a treat for any positive interaction with the tunnel, like rubbing their face on it or going inside.

2. Place the target stick a few inches inside the tunnel. Click and treat when your cat targets.

3. Extend the target stick farther into the tunnel. You may need to get on the opposite end of the tunnel. Click and treat each time your cat makes it through the tunnel.

4. Once your cat is comfortable going through the tunnel, position them at one end and say "tunnel," and hold your target stick at the far end of the tunnel. Click and treat for going through. Repeat this step five or six times.

5. Once your cat walks through with just the verbal cue, slowly limit the use of the target stick. Start by briefly showing the target stick, say "tunnel," and then remove the stick as your cat walks through the tunnel. Click and treat for each successful tunnel walk-through.

PRO TIP

If your cat won't target through the tunnel, use a wand feather cat toy to encourage them through it. Phase this out quickly; otherwise, your cat will think you're just trying to play with them.

Hurdle Jump

We're raising the bar, literally! Hurdles are a great activity to help your cat burn off excess energy and get in some exercise. This hurdle can also be used as part of a cat agility course at home. Anything can be used as a hurdle. This exercise will show you how to train your cat using common items found around the home.

DURATION 5 minutes, twice a day until trained

MATERIALS

🐾 Broomstick

🐾 Clicker

🐾 Your cat's favorite treats

🐾 Two small boxes (such as shoeboxes)

🐾 Tape

🐾 Target stick

1. Lay a broomstick flat on the ground. Have your cat follow the target stick over the top of the broomstick. Click and reward them with a treat. Repeat this step five or six times.

2. Raise the broomstick one to two inches off the ground, using shoebox lids or other items to lift it up. Tape the broomstick in place so it won't roll. Use your target stick to motion your cat toward the top of the broomstick. Click and treat as they step over the broomstick.

3. Raise the broomstick a few more inches by securing it on top of the shoeboxes. Click and treat each time the cat successfully follows the target over the top of the broomstick.

4. As your cat gets more comfortable, continue to raise the height of the broomstick using more or bigger boxes. At some point, your cat will need to jump to follow the target over

the broomstick. Give them a jackpot (see Pro Tip, page 45) the first time this happens.

5. Once your cat is consistently following the target by jumping over the broomstick, start adding in a verbal cue of "hurdle" right before your cat jumps. Click and treat.

6. Fade out the use of the target stick once your cat jumps over the hurdle whenever you say "hurdle." To do this, slowly decrease the target stick movements. Go at your cat's pace so you don't confuse them by removing the target stick. If your cat seems confused, go back to step 5 to strengthen the association with the verbal cue "hurdle."

PRO TIP

Make sure the broomstick is secured to whatever item it's suspended on so it doesn't roll off or fall if your cat touches it.

Magic Cup Game

In this game, you'll engage your cat as they learn to pay attention to where you placed the treat and where it was moved to. This is great mental stimulation for kitty—and hilarious to watch.

DURATION   5 minutes, twice a day until trained

MATERIALS

- 🐾 Two to four opaque cups, walnut shells, or bottle caps
- 🐾 Clicker
- 🐾 Your cat's favorite treats

1. Place the cups in a line in front of your cat. Let your cat sniff and see the treat in your hand.

2. Place the treat underneath one of the cups but don't move the cup. Click and reward them with a treat when your cat paws or nudges the cup with the treat underneath it.

3. Repeat this process 10 times, alternating which cup the treat is under but not moving the cup around. Click and treat for each correct choice by your cat.

4. Now, place a treat under a cup and slowly move it around. When starting out, you want to move it only a few inches, but you can increase the movement once your cat gets the hang of it. Click and treat if your cat paws or sniffs the correct cup.

5. Work your way up to moving the cups around more, moving them faster, and swapping their locations. Click and treat for each correct choice.

PRO TIP

Once your cat has the game down, swap the treat out for a small ball for them to find. This way, they won't have the advantage of smell to find the right cup.

Chair Leaps

Once your cat knows this trick, you can transfer this skill to other platforms, including smaller stools. All of this activity is great exercise for your cat and a fun way to use furniture in your house for training. Make sure the chairs you use are stable so they don't topple or scare your cat into abandoning their acrobatic aspirations.

DURATION 5 minutes, twice a day until trained

MATERIALS

- 🐾 Two chairs
- 🐾 Target stick
- 🐾 Clicker
- 🐾 Your cat's favorite treats

1. Place two chairs directly next to each other, with no gap in between. Use the target stick to signal your cat to jump onto one of the chairs. Click and reward them with a treat.

2. Using the target stick, motion your cat to move from one chair to the other. Click and treat.

3. Now, move one chair an inch away from the other. Target your cat from chair to chair. Click and treat for each successful target.

4. Slowly increase the distance between the chairs, inch by inch. Target back and forth, clicking and treating for each successful target.

5. Eventually, your cat will need to jump to get from one chair to the other. Reward with a jackpot (see Pro Tip, page 45) the first time your cat successfully jumps from one chair to the other.

6. Slowly fade out the target stick to a finger cue by pointing to the chair. Your cat will now associate your finger pointing to a chair as the cue to jump to it. Click and treat for each successful jump.

PRO TIP

After you fade out the target stick and replace it with your finger pointing, your cat may need an occasional refresher to jump using the target stick.

Figure Eight Leg Weave

This skill is challenging, but it's still a fun game to play with your cat. The goal here is to train your cat how to do a figure eight around your legs while you're standing still, or train them to weave while you're walking. Once they master this, you can even have them weave to the beat of the music as you walk.

DURATION   5 minutes, twice a day until trained

MATERIALS

- 🐾 Your cat's favorite treats
- 🐾 Target stick
- 🐾 Clicker

1. Stand with your legs spread slightly more than shoulder-width apart. Get your cat used to walking underneath your legs by tossing some treats on the floor below you. Clicking isn't necessary yet.

2. Using your target stick, signal your cat to go from in front of you, through the middle of your legs, and then around to the side of one leg. Click and reward them with a treat. Make sure to give the treat in front of you so your cat knows to come back to the front starting position after they go through your legs.

3. Once your cat is used to going under your legs following the target, remove the target stick from between your legs. Instead, place it by the side of your leg you want them to go around. Click and treat them in front of you after they go through your legs. This will test if your cat knows how to walk between your legs and around to the target stick. If they don't understand yet, keep repeating step 2 until they do.

4. Repeat steps 1 to 3 for each individual leg until they've mastered it.

5. Now, signal your cat to walk around both legs in a figure eight shape before you click and treat. Use the target stick to motion your cat around one leg and then again around the other. Click as soon as your cat goes around your second leg and give them a treat in front of you.

6. Fade out the use of the target stick and replace with a pointed finger. (If you have a retractable target stick, you can make it shorter over time until your pointed finger is the replacement.) Use your finger to point to the leg you want your cat to weave around as the cue. Only click and treat after your cat has completed the entire figure eight. Continue to give treats in front of you after a successful figure eight.

7. Now, take a few steps, using your finger to point to your forward leg for a walking figure eight leg weave. Click and give them a treat in front of you for each successful walking weave. At first, smaller steps may be easier for you and your cat, but you can upgrade as they progress.

8. Fade out the finger-pointing cue until the natural motion of your leg stepping forward signals your cat to weave underneath your leg. Click and treat for each successful weave.

PRO TIP

If your cat tries to move around the outside of your legs instead of through the middle, widen your stance to encourage them to go directly under your legs.

CHAPTER 7

COOL CAT TRICKS

The tricks you are about to learn are sure to grab everyone's attention. This chapter covers some more fun (and unusual) skills that you can train your cat to do. These behaviors are especially fun to show off when you have friends over. They'll all love your little "party animal"!

Roll Over

Does your cat know how to lie down on command (page 46)? If so, wow your friends with a cat who can roll over! When training this skill, you will need to keep your cat's comfort in mind. Practicing on carpet instead of a hard floor will prevent discomfort. Older cats with limited mobility may not be able to do this trick. As with the Spin Around trick (page 96), train this skill in one direction first before going through the steps on the other side.

DURATION 5 minutes, twice a day until trained

MATERIALS

🐾 Your cat's favorite treats

🐾 Clicker

1. With your cat in front of you, ask them to lie down. If your cat lies down on their side with one hip touching the floor, click and reward them with a treat.

2. If your cat lies down in a "sphinx" position, you'll need to get them used to lying on their hip. To do this, hold a treat in your hand and slowly move the hand with the treat near the side of their head toward their back legs. Click and treat as soon as your cat relaxes onto their hip.

3. Next, get your cat to rest their shoulder on the ground. With a treat in your hand, move your hand toward your cat's neck and shoulder area. Click as soon as your cat's opposite shoulder touches the ground. Try to feed your cat the treat in this position.

4. Now, you'll begin training the actual roll. With a treat in your hand, move your hand near your cat's neck from one side of their body toward the other. Click and treat.

5. If your cat didn't roll all the way over, click and give them a treat for rolling as far as they

go. Keep working on it, inch by inch, until your cat rolls all the way over. The first time your cat rolls all the way over, give them a jackpot (see Pro Tip, page 45).

6. Fade out from using the food in your hand to just a hand cue. With your finger pointed, move your finger in a half-circle motion over your cat's head.

Start feeding the treat from your opposite hand so your cat stops thinking that the hand with the cue is supposed to have treats. Click and treat for each successful roll.

7. Once your cat knows how to roll over in one direction, return to step 1 to train them in the opposite direction.

PRO TIP

When learning how to roll over, your cat may use their paws to grab your hands. This is fine as long as their claws aren't out. They're trying to stabilize themselves since they don't have enough momentum to roll all the way over yet. You can help them succeed!

Spin Around

This behavior involves training your cat to turn around in a circle. When training them to spin, it's important to teach moving in one direction in its entirety before you train going in the opposite direction to avoid confusing your cat.

DURATION 5 minutes, twice a day until trained

MATERIALS

🐾 Target stick

🐾 Clicker

🐾 Your cat's favorite treats

1. With your cat in front of you, motion the target stick in a half circle away from you so that they'll turn slightly to their right to follow it. Click and toss a treat in a spot that will help them complete the full turn. This will help your cat get comfortable completing the spin movement from the beginning of the training session.

2. Repeat step 1 until your cat knows how to do the full spin following the target stick.

3. Start fading out the use of the target stick and replace it with a pointed finger as the cue. This can be done by extending a pointed finger on the same hand that's holding the target stick. Slowly shorten the target stick while continuing to point with your finger. Eventually the target stick will be the same length as your finger and will no longer be needed.

4. Once the target stick is no longer being used, your cat should be able to spin in one direction by following your finger in a spinning motion toward the direction you are signaling. Click and treat for a full spin completion.

5. Return to step 1 and teach your cat to spin in the opposite direction.

PRO TIP

Once your cat knows how to spin around once (both ways), you can ask them to spin once in either direction before clicking and giving a treat for a figure eight.

High Five

This cat trick will train your cool kitty to give a high five to anyone who asks. If you want to celebrate an accomplishment (or just need a boost), your furry friend will be able to share in your joy!

DURATION   5 minutes, twice a day until trained

MATERIALS

🐾 Your cat's favorite treats

🐾 Clicker

1. Hold a treat in your hand. Hold that hand slightly above your cat's head with your palm facing out. Click and give them a treat from your other hand when your cat sticks their paw up to grab the treat.

2. Continue this process five to ten times, but only click if your cat doesn't have their claws out. You don't want them to think you're asking them to claw your hand.

3. Now, remove the treat from your high-five hand. Click and treat for each successful high five.

4. Add in the verbal cue "high five" immediately before you put your hand out for a high five. Click and give them a treat if they actually connect. Continue to do this until your cat begins to high-five you consistently.

PRO TIP

If your cat jumps up to get your hand, you're probably holding your hand too high above their head. Make sure your hand is easily accessible for them when they're sitting on their hind legs.

Sitting Pretty

This pose will have your cat sitting on their hind legs, with their back erect and front legs up off the floor. This is a great pose to show how adorable and well-behaved your cat is on social media.

DURATION   5 minutes, twice a day until trained

MATERIALS

🐾 Your cat's favorite treats

🐾 Clicker

🐾 Target stick

1. Hold a treat above your cat's head so they have to sit up on their hind legs. Once your cat's front paws are up in the air, click and reward them with the treat while they're in that upright position.

2. Grab four or five treats and persuade your cat to sit up so they're resting on their two hind legs again. Click and treat, keeping them in this position until all the treats in your hand are gone. Repeat this process a few times to get your cat comfortable holding this upright position.

3. After you're out of the treats from your hand, click as soon as your cat's front feet touch the ground again. Give them another treat.

4. Next, use a target stick held above your cat's head to get them into the sitting pretty position. Click and treat. Repeat this until your cat reliably follows the target stick up into the pose.

5. Start fading out the target stick to just a hand cue of your finger, pointed up toward the ceiling. Fade out the target stick by making it smaller over time until your cat is sitting pretty with only the hand cue. Click and treat for each successful "sitting pretty."

PRO TIP

If your cat tries to grab the target stick, quickly click before they're able to. Then give them a treat. It's easier to cut out the grabbing behavior by clicking before the behavior happens than to get your cat to let go of the target stick.

Kitty Kisses

Do you wish your cat showed more affection? The following steps will show you how to train your cat to give you "kisses" by getting your cat to target their face to your cheek. This is also a great photo op or trick to show off to others.

DURATION 5 minutes, twice a day until trained

MATERIALS

🐾 Target stick

🐾 Clicker

🐾 Your cat's favorite treats

1. While sitting on the floor, hold the target stick to your shoulder. Click when your cat targets and reward them with a treat.

2. Slowly move the target inch by inch, clicking and treating, until the target is against your cheek.

3. Continue to hold the target to your cheek and have your cat target about 10 times before continuing on. Click and treat for each successful target.

4. Fade out the target stick to using your finger, pointing to your cheek. Click and treat for each phase of fading until your cat is targeting your cheek using only your pointed finger.

5. Once your cat "kisses" your cheek using only the finger cue, you can add in a verbal cue of "kiss." To do this, say "kiss" and then immediately give the finger cue. Click and treat.

6. Continue step 5 as many times as necessary while you fade out the finger cue. Eventually you'll be able to say the word "kiss" and have your cat come over and give you a kiss on the cheek. Click and treat for each successful kiss.

PRO TIP

I don't recommend putting wet cat food on your cheek (like you'll find in some recommendations online). You want kisses, not hungry "love bites"!

Waving Hello

To learn this trick, your cat should already be familiar with how to station on a mat (page 44) and how to give you a high five (page 97). Whenever someone waves at your cat, they'll now receive a friendly wave back!

DURATION   5 minutes, twice a day until trained

MATERIALS

🐾 Mat for station

🐾 Clicker

🐾 Your cat's favorite treats

1. Start with your cat stationed on a mat. Click and reward them with a treat for staying on the mat.

2. Click and treat your cat as they stay on the mat while you step back a few feet and move around.

3. With your cat on the mat, come over to them and hold your hand up in the same position that you ask for a high five, except don't give a verbal cue. Click and treat if your cat gives you a high five.

4. Next, hold your hand up again, but click before your cat's paw touches your hand. Give them a treat. Repeat this process 10 times or more. Your cat should be raising their paw, but not touching your hand.

5. Slowly start moving your hand farther away from your cat, inch by inch. Click and treat each time your cat raises their paw. Take this step slowly, and repeat it numerous times. You want your cat to stay on their mat and not follow you.

6. Once your cat is staying on the mat and waving while you're a few feet away, add in the hand cue. Instead of holding your hand up motionless, add in

a slight wave. Click and treat for each completed wave from your cat. Make sure they're still staying on the mat.

7. Once your cat is used to the waving hand cue, you can add in a verbal cue of "hi." Say "hi" immediately before you give the hand cue for the wave. Click and treat for each wave your cat does.

PRO TIP

If your cat keeps getting off their mat, place the mat on a chair or stool. This way, they'll be more likely to stay on it rather than follow you.

Keyboard Kitty

Train your cat to play the piano! With practice, you can train your cat to play certain notes, but we'll start their musical career by training them to press random keys on a piano. The following steps use a toy piano, but cats are awesome and can be easily trained on a full-size one, too. They'll just need a bench so they can reach the keys.

DURATION   5 minutes, twice a day until trained

MATERIALS

- 🐾 Toy piano or full-size piano with bench
- 🐾 Target stick
- 🐾 Clicker
- 🐾 Your cat's favorite treats

1. Place the toy piano on the ground in front of you and your cat. Let your cat explore the piano. Gently press one of the piano keys so they begin to understand the noises the piano makes.

2. Hold the target stick over the piano, in a place where your cat will need to step on a piano key. As soon as your cat steps one front foot on a key to reach the target, click and reward them with a treat.

3. Keep repeating step 2 until your cat is comfortable stepping on the keys. Click and give them a treat each time.

4. Add in the verbal cue of "play" immediately before showing the target stick. Click and treat as soon as your cat plays a note.

5. Fade out using the target stick over time to just using the verbal cue, clicking and treating for pressing the keys. Your cat should know to touch the piano key after hearing the verbal cue "play."

PRO TIP

If your cat is afraid of the noise the piano makes, you can use an electronic keyboard that lets you lower the volume.

Jumping Through an Arm Hoop

This is the trademark maneuver of a well-trained circus cat. If you want your friends to be uber impressed with your training skills, this is the behavior to show.

DURATION   5 minutes, twice a day until trained

MATERIALS

🐾 Clicker

🐾 Your cat's favorite treats

1. Place a treat in one hand. With your arms outstretched, place the non-treat hand against a wall, low enough for your cat to easily jump over.

2. With your cat on one side of you, persuade them to jump over your arm using the treat hand. Click as your cat jumps over your arm and reward them with a treat.

3. Fade out using the treat to lead your cat over your arm by pointing your finger. Click and treat for each successful jump.

4. Now, fade out your finger as the cue. You want your cat to jump over as soon as your arm is placed with your palm against the wall. Click and treat.

5. With your one arm as the hurdle, place the palm of your other hand a few feet higher on the wall. This arm will become the top of the hoop. Click and treat for each successful jump.

6. Slowly move your upper arm down, moving closer to your lower arm to make a hoop. Click and treat for each successful jump.

7. Continue to close the distance until your hands can interlock in a hoop shape. Keep practicing with your hands against the wall. Click and treat for each successful jump.

8. Slowly move your arm hoop a few inches away from the wall, then work your way up to greater distances, different body positions, and varying heights. Click and treat for each successful jump.

PRO TIP

You can use your tongue to make a click sound instead of the mechanical clicker.

RESOURCES

I hope you'll keep learning and training your cat. There's still a lot we don't know about animals, so don't ever think your cat can't do something just because they haven't done it before! The following resources will help in continuing your cat's training.

Websites

Cat Training Supplies: CuriosityTrained.com/cat-training-tools

This is a list of recommended cat training tools.

Free Training Planner: CuriosityTrained.com/book-training-planner

This is my free planner for organizing and planning your cat training sessions.

Best Cat Harnesses and Leashes: CuriosityTrained.com/best-cat-harness

Here are my favorite harnesses and leashes for cats.

Tips for Choosing a Cat Brush: CuriosityTrained.com/best-cat-brush

Here you'll learn how to choose the right cat brush.

Cat Puzzle Feeder Recommendations: CuriosityTrained.com /interactive-cat-puzzle-toys

Here is a list of puzzle feeders I recommend.

Clicker Training Terms and Knowledge Building: ClickerTraining.com /library

> *Build your cat training vocabulary with this library of terms and information.*

Additional Clicker Training Concepts: StaleCheerios.com/top-blog-posts

> *Here you'll find articles for expanding your clicker training knowledge.*

Beyond Training—Learn about Cat Enrichment: CuriosityTrained.com /cat-enrichment-guide

> *This guide teaches about how to make sure your cat is never bored again!*

Books

Don't Shoot the Dog by Karen Pryor

> *A great training book to read once you finish this one.*

Reaching the Animal Mind by Karen Pryor

> *This book contains interesting stories about clicker training across species.*

REFERENCES

American Association of Feline Practitioners. "Feline Behavior
    Guidelines." Accessed December 20, 2020. CatVets.com/public
    /PDFs/PracticeGuidelines/FelineBehaviorGLS.pdf.

Ault, Alicia. "Ask Smithsonian: Are Cats Domesticated?"
    Smithsonian Magazine. April 30, 2015. SmithsonianMag
    .com/smithsonian-institution/ask-smithsonian-are-cats
    -domesticated-180955111.

Driscoll, Carlos A., Juliet Clutton-Brock, Andrew C. Kitchener, and Stephen J.
    O'Brien. "The Taming of the Cat." *Scientific American* 300, no. 6 (2009):
    68–75. ncbi.nlm.nih.gov/pmc/articles/PMC5790555.

Ghose, Tia. "Feline Vision: How Cats See the World." *Live Science*.
    October 16, 2013. LiveScience.com/40459-what-do-cats-see.html.

Litchfield, Carla A., Gillian Quinton, Hayley Tindele, Belinda Chiera,
    K. Heidy Kikillus, and Philip Roetman. "The 'Feline Five': An
    Exploration of Personality in Pet Cats (*Felis catus*)." *PLOS ONE* 12,
    no. 8 (August 23, 2017): e0183455. doi:10.1371/journal.pone.0183455.

McLeod, Saul. "Edward Thorndike: The Law of Effect." *Simply Psychology*
    (blog). Updated 2018. SimplyPsychology.org/edward-thorndike.html.

McLeod, Saul. "What Is Operant Conditioning and How Does It Work?"
    Simply Psychology (blog). Updated 2018. SimplyPsychology.org
    /operant-conditioning.html.

Pryor, Karen. *Don't Shoot the Dog.* Rev. ed. Lydney, Gloucestershire: Ringpress Books, Ltd., 2002.

Ramirez, Ken. "Animal Training: Successful Animal Management Through Positive Reinforcement." Chicago: Shedd Aquarium Society, 1999.

SNL. "More Cowbell." YouTube. Accessed February 20, 2021. YouTube .com/watch?v=cVsQLlk-T0s.

Sunquist, Mel, and Fiona Sunquist. *Wild Cats of the World.* Chicago: University of Chicago Press, 2002.

Vieira de Castro, Ana Catarina, Danielle Fuchs, Gabriela Munhoz Morello, Stefania Pastur, Liliana de Sousa, and Anna S. Olsson. "Does Training Method Matter?: Evidence for the Negative Impact of Aversive-Based Methods on Companion Dog Welfare." *PLOS ONE* 15, no. 12 (December 16, 2020): e0225023. doi:10.1371/journal.pone.0225023.

INDEX

Acknowledgments

I want to start by thanking my amazing husband, CJ. He has always been there cheering me on as I chased after my dream of becoming a carnivore keeper and working with cheetahs. From keeping our son entertained for many, many weekends so I could write, to encouraging me to keep going, I couldn't have completed this book without him.

Special thanks to my son, whose unadulterated love for animals continues to ignite my joy.

To Lizzy and Katie, thanks for being part of my carnivore crew. Bouncing ideas off of fellow training nerds helped me grow into the trainer that I am today. Thanks for sticking by me all those years with your friendship. I'm truly lucky to be able to call you my friends.

Thanks to all the keepers I've worked with over the years. I've learned something from each and every one of you and am fortunate to have spent over 12 years working in this field.

Additional thanks to Callisto Media for taking the chance on publishing this book and to Samantha Holland for walking me through the entire process.

About the Author

 **STEPHANIE MANTILLA** is a positive reinforcement-based animal trainer with over 15 years of experience. She spent over 12 years as a zookeeper and trained a little bit of everything, including sloths, monkeys, rhinos, bears, cheetahs, cougars, and much more.

One of Stephanie's favorite animals is the cheetah, and in 2013, she traveled to Namibia to spend time volunteering at the Cheetah Conservation Fund. Before she left her position as a senior carnivore keeper at the Houston Zoo, Stephanie was her department's training and enrichment coordinator. She has a BS in biology and environmental science and received a behavioral husbandry certificate from the Association of Zoos and Aquariums. Stephanie now runs her own business that focuses on training domestic cats and dogs using clicker training. She helps cat parents enhance their cat's life on her website, CuriosityTrained.com.